HOW MULTIMEDIA WORKS

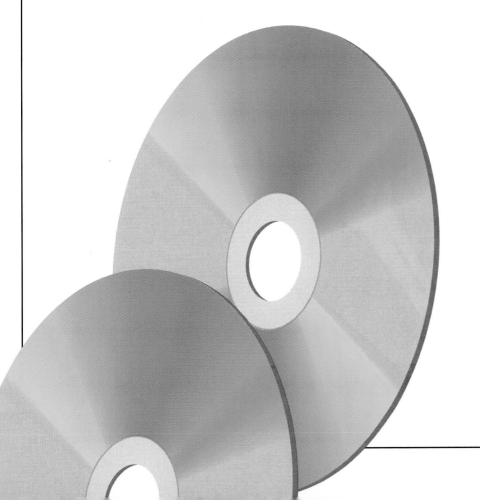

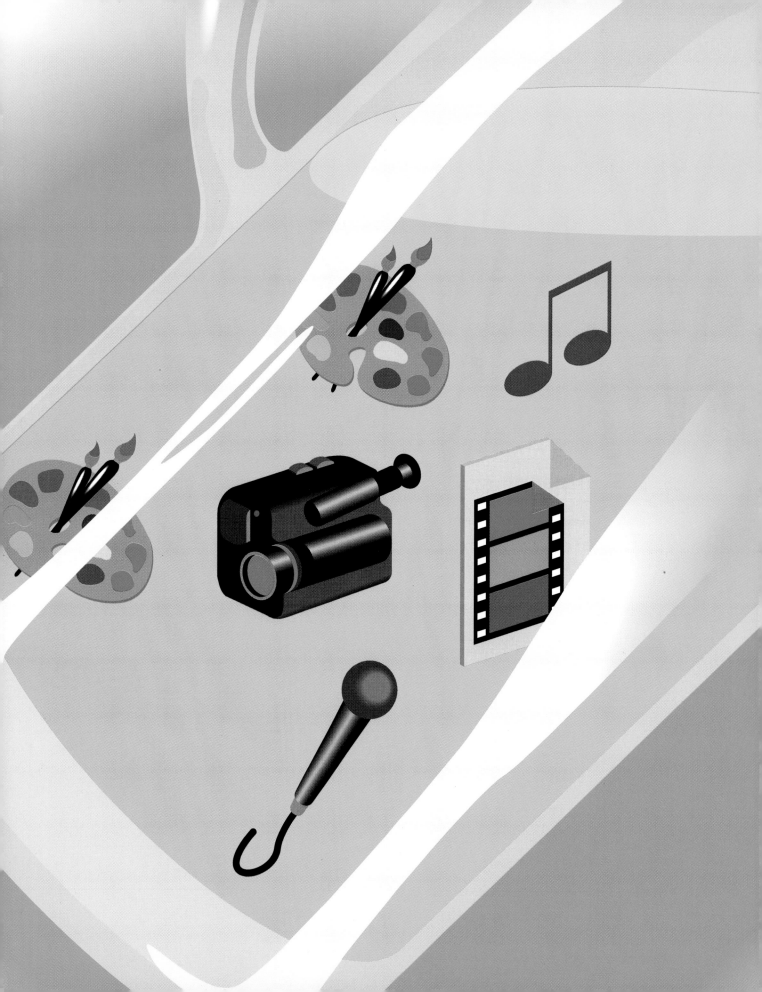

HOW MULTIMEDIA WORKS

ERIK HOLSINGER

Illustrated by
NEVIN BERGER

Ziff-Davis Press
Emeryville, California

Development Editor	Valerie Haynes Perry
Copy Editor	Jan Jue
Technical Reviewer	David Lawrence
Project Coordinator	Barbara Dahl
Proofreader	Carol Burbo
Cover Illustration	Nevin Berger and Regan Honda
Cover Design	Carrie English
Series Book Design	Carrie English
Illustrator	Nevin Berger
Word Processor	Howard Blechman
Layout Artist	Tony Jonick
Digital Prepress Specialist	Joe Schneider
Indexer	Valerie Robbins

Ziff-Davis Press books are produced on a Macintosh computer system with the following applications: FrameMaker®, Microsoft® Word, QuarkXPress®, Adobe Illustrator®, Adobe Photoshop®, Adobe Streamline™, MacLink®*Plus*, Aldus® FreeHand™, Collage Plus™.

If you have comments or questions or would like to receive a free catalog, call or write:
Ziff-Davis Press
5903 Christie Avenue
Emeryville, CA 94608
1-800-688-0448

ISBN 1-56276-208-7

Manufactured in the United States of America
♲ This book is printed on paper that contains 50% total recycled fiber of which 20% is de-inked postconsumer fiber.
10 9 8 7 6 5 4 3 2 1

This book is for my parents,
Lloyd and Eve Holsinger,
whose love and support have
never wavered, even when
they weren't sure exactly
what they were supporting.
Since they never actually
asked, I thought I would
finally answer the one question I'm sure has pestered
them these many years.
Here goes:

Dear Mom and Dad:
This is what I do for a living.
Love, Erik

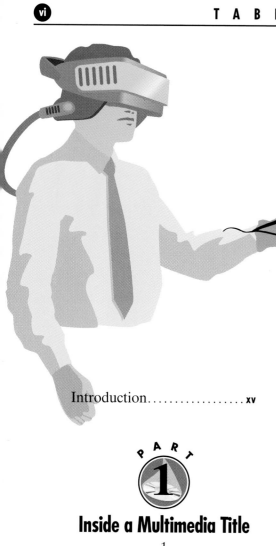

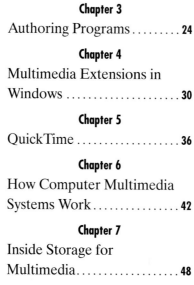

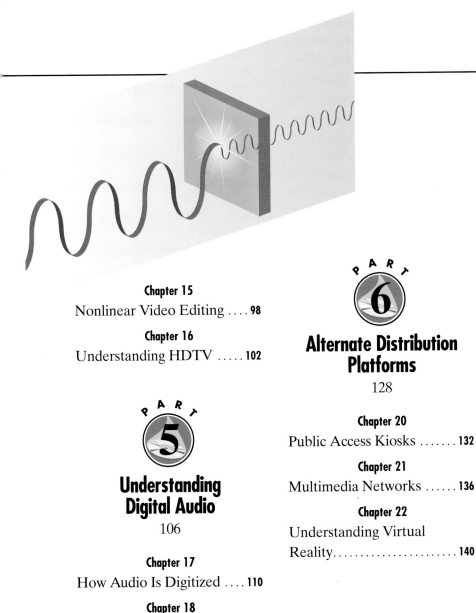

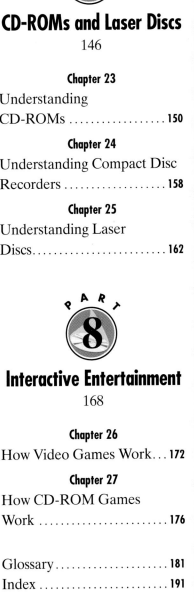

Think of yourself as a multimedia machine. Sometime today, you will probably try to explain something to somebody else. You might give directions to your house, or describe a product to a potential customer. Multimedia is a new way to explain and understand things.

Because multimedia computing is a new concept to most of us, it would be nice if someone would explain it clearly. But there is a curious gap among publications about computers. On the one hand there are books for "dummies," which explain what a disk is and how to insert it into a slot. Then there are the programming manuals that assume the reader is familiar with bubble sorts and clock rates. We really need more books that are in between, which give the reader a little credit for intelligence, yet are not afraid to explain complex topics simply and clearly. That's what Erik Holsinger has provided here.

First of all, he's a good explainer. That's what impressed me when I read his book, *MacWEEK Guide to Desktop Video*. And this rare talent and ability impressed me when I first met him at a symposium on multimedia at San Francisco State University. When you listen to him, or read his books, it's clear that he knows as much or more than you do about video production and multimedia. But it's also clear that he wants you to learn. And he is so enthusiastic that he will do anything to make sure you "get it."

I "got" something out of every chapter of *How Multimedia Works*. This book is part of that great series of How It Works titles from Ziff-Davis Press. I like the rich illustrations, easy pace, and the occasional step back for perspective that is characteristic of this series. I've never seen digital compression explained as well as Erik explains it in Chapter 13, *Understanding JPEG Compression*. And HDTV becomes more than just an acronym for high-definition television in Chapter 16.

There are writers who report and writers who repeat; Erik Holsinger is a writer who can explain.

Richard Hart
Host
The Next Step on The Discovery Channel

Without a doubt, I owe the greatest thanks to my friend Nevin Berger, the phenomenal artist who created all the illustrations in this book. Nevin's incredible artistic skills and his wonderful sense of humor made the production of this book an absolute pleasure. Over the many months that we worked together, Nevin never failed to transform my crude sketches and layouts into concise works of art. Yet despite the pressures of a full-time job, buying a new house, and having twins, Nevin never let his enthusiasm or steady stream of corny jokes wind down. I salute you, Infographic Specialist del Mundo!

Many people at Ziff-Davis Press were also invaluable in bringing this book together. Cindy Hudson, the president of Ziff-Davis Press, deserves a round of applause for her persistence in trying to get me to write this book. Her publishing savvy, sense of humor, and commitment to doing good work make it always a pleasure to work with her.

I was honored to again work with Valerie Haynes Perry and Jan Jue. Valerie was the development editor and Jan the copy editor on this book, and both were essential to maintaining my style and focus throughout the book. The clarity of the text is a tribute to their candor, patience, and skill. Barbara Dahl, the project coordinator for this book, helped keep everything together when the text finally made it to final page proofs, as well as keeping track of all the last-minute corrections and additions.

Many thanks go to the Ziff-Davis Press art production staff (Elisabeth Beller, Tony Jonick, Joe Schneider, Dan Brodnitz, and Charles Cowens). Joe, Dan, and Charley handled all the color pre-press work, which is no small job for a book filled with wall-to-wall illustrations. Tony beautifully integrated my text with Nevin's artwork in page layouts, as well as gracing each image with a variety of aptly placed gradient blends. As usual, Elisabeth coordinated all the art production on the project with an effortless precision that borders on superhuman.

My thanks and sincere apologies to Howard Blechman who did the word processing on the book, and had to suffer through my arcane handwritten corrections.

I had the great fortune to work with my good friend David Lawrence, a phenomenal artist and multimedia producer in San Francisco. As this book's technical editor, David drew on his vast experience, honesty, and commitment to clarity to provide me with vital feedback. Dave showed me time and again that nothing is ever really wrong; it's just badly designed.

Much of this book contains technical information gathered from dozens of different sources over the years. While space doesn't permit me to thank all concerned, I'd like to especially thank several people who were vital to the completion of this book. Kudos to:

Helayne Waldman Smith, a multimedia instructor based in the San Francisco Bay Area, who provided invaluable feedback on this book as I was working up the outline; the indomitable Linda

Jacobson, an excellent writer and one of the foremost experts in virtual reality technology in the country, who helped me get a handle on my chapter on virtual reality technology; Steve Gano at Kaleida Labs, who patiently talked me through the details of ScriptX, and who took the time to look at proofs even while trying to finish production on their software; Karen Curcio of Curcio and Company, who managed to get me detailed information on IBM's latest multimedia hardware systems; Frank Colin at Equilibrium Software, who provided custom software for re-creating the different image palettes used in the graphics chapter; and Kord Taylor at Opcode Systems, who helped clarify details on digital audio and MIDI.

The chapters on video games would not have been possible without the help of Kris Gilbert of Manning Selvage & Lee, Sega's public relations agency, and Rick Reynolds at 3DO Corporation. Despite hard-core company policies of "that's for us to know and you to find out," both Kris and Rick managed to get me detailed hardware information on both the Sega Genesis and 3DO player.

Michael W. Zak, the marketing manager for Colorbytes, Inc., deserves special thanks for allowing us to use a variety of gorgeous photos from the Colorbytes Image Library. These photos from Colorbytes Sampler One and Two added an extra pizzazz to several spreads. Gina Cercucia and Dave Laurer of ASDG were invaluable in providing images for morphing and warping; Dave also created the great morphing example using ASDG's Elastic Reality software.

The many months that it takes to write a book can be very rough on friendships. I'd like to thank my good friends, especially Joan and John Starkovich, Robby and Mabel Robbins, Andres Sender, David Hopkins, Polly Smith, Robert Luhn, Bill Meese, Georgie Lee Able, Yoshi Stewart, and Karen Wickre, for being so patient, caring, and supportive while I went into "Deadline Hell" mode during the writing of this book. I would never have been able to complete this book without them.

Finally, I'd like to thank Suzanne Anthony for showing me that there really is life after multimedia—and a grand one at that.

When Cindy Hudson, the president of Ziff-Davis Press, first asked me if I wanted to write a book called *How Multimedia Works*, I had to laugh before saying no. She patiently waited until I stopped chuckling and then asked, "Okay, why not?"

"Because it'll be a really short book," I said. "Just the title, my byline, and a single line that says 'It doesn't. The End.'"

Admittedly I had become a little jaded. As an independent multimedia producer, I'm one of many people who has endured poor software programs, hardware that doesn't quite do the job, and a market that seems to be made of 90 percent inert gases and 10 percent fact. I just didn't see how I could provide anything other than pages of multimedia angst.

However, Cindy's determination, as well as her ability to definitively articulate a good argument finally paid off: We debated the value of this book off and on for about eight months, when I finally agreed that I would at least research the marketplace. As it turns out, she was right—there was a book that we needed to do.

I found that there isn't a book out there that is just for consumers—all the regular folks who are supposedly the main buying audience for multimedia programs. True, if you want to produce multimedia titles, there are over a dozen books that cover everything you need to know for specific programs and platforms. Yet most of my friends and family don't work with computers and multimedia technology on a regular basis, so those books wouldn't provide the information they need in an easy-to-understand way.

How Multimedia Works is for anyone who wants to understand what all the noise about multimedia really means, regardless of how much computer experience you may have or how familiar you are with multimedia technology. I've tried to keep the text jargon-free, while explaining key concepts in an easy, conversational style. In addition to covering basic concepts, I've included production notes that offer inside information on what producers have to keep in mind when creating titles. Finally, this book uses a variety of graphics that will give you a detailed overview of the market place and the current technology behind multimedia. It will also give you a good idea of what you can expect from this technology in the future.

Erik Holsinger
San Francisco, California
May 17, 1994

INSIDE A MULTIMEDIA TITLE

CONTENTS

CALL IT WHAT YOU WILL: multimedia, new media, integrated media, or even muddy media. I doubt that there has ever been a term as convoluted, overrated, or misunderstood.

When professionals in the computer industry talk about multimedia, they mention the collision of the communication, entertainment, and computer industries. Those same professionals are never exactly sure whether the result of this collision is a computer or a consumer product. Despite the fact that there isn't a multimedia delivery system as standard as a VCR, every major consumer electronic giant insists that multimedia belongs in the realm of the consumer. This explains the scramble to bring to market flashy new multimedia machines that are projected to be a bigger industry than the $3+ billion video game market.

With this much money flying around, the entertainment industry was bound to get involved. Newspapers are constantly running stories of Hollywood movie studios working frantically to develop big deals to create multimedia titles. Most folks at these studios couldn't even begin to tell you what a multimedia program or title is, but you better believe that whatever it is, they'll have one before the competition.

To add to the confusion, no one seems to really know the extent of the multimedia market. Newspapers and magazines will report the latest findings of "multimedia analysts," who announce gloriously outrageous market figures every week, in which it is certain that by the year 2000 the multimedia market will be a $650 billion industry (give or take $650 billion). The amazing thing is that there are so few hard facts about the number of people who actually buy multimedia hardware and software.

The ultimate costs in using multimedia products are hard to estimate. Not only do different systems need enhanced (and often expensive) hardware and software, but even then not all multimedia programs can run on all types of machines. Yet the computer industry insists that multimedia will be the way that the general public gets involved in computing—even if you have to add thousands of dollars onto the price of your computer system in order to play a single multimedia title that you bought for $29.

Paradoxes like these cause people in the financial markets to shake their heads, wondering why there is so much excitement about multimedia when it appears that no one is making any money. Yet it seems to be getting more pervasive every year. Why? The answer is simple. Despite all the confusion, all the outrageous claims, there is a truth hidden behind the hype, a substantial *something* to all this that causes hardened cynics like myself to pause before writing the whole industry off as an elaborate hoax. In a word, multimedia hs great *potential*.

Multimedia has the potential to be one of the most powerful forms of communicating ideas, searching for information, and experiencing new concepts of any communication media ever developed. This is simply because multimedia *incorporates* every type of media ever developed.

Television, film, graphic art, books, magazines, radio, animation—some of the better elements from all of these media are a part of multimedia projects. And that's where the real potential lies; a truly outstanding multimedia title could potentially provide an even better experience than any of the other media could individually.

Multimedia adds one important aspect to the mix: interactivity. Interactivity is the key element in defining multimedia. Many people will say that multimedia combines sound, video, graphics, and text; yet they could just as easily be describing television. Every night on the news you see a combination of all of these elements, but you wouldn't call it multimedia, because you can't interact with it (other than switching the channel). A multimedia version of a newscast could contain all of the elements of the newscast, but you'd be the one who tells the newscaster what information you want to hear and when you want to hear it. The choice is yours. Just click a button, touch a screen, or press down on a keyboard, and you can call the shots within the multimedia title.

Aside from sheer potential, the technology available today is another reason for the excitement about multimedia. At present we are able to combine all current media more smoothly than ever, using technology at a price that wasn't dreamed of just ten years ago. Producers created multimedia presentations as far back as the early 1980s. The main difference is that back then it took months and cost hundreds of thousands of dollars to do projects that today can be done in half the time and at a fraction of the cost.

As current technologies continue to improve, software sophistication increases, and hardware gets cheaper to build, the potential for multimedia machines to become as common as your VCR is greater than ever. No wonder the computer, entertainment, cable, telecommunications, and other major consumer electronic industries are racing to develop this emerging market.

This section will give you examples of how multimedia is used today, and how it will be used in the future, to give you a better idea of its potential. This framework will help you put all of the technologies discussed in this book into a reasonable context, and perhaps help you understand what all the excitement is about.

How Multimedia Fits into Your Life

ONE OF THE MAIN reasons multimedia is such a mystery to the general public is that there are so few examples of multimedia products. Yet multimedia continues to creep into our lives as entertainment and information become available in digital formats. As with most early technologies, there are just a few businesses, educational institutions, and entertainment houses that have created successful products with multimedia technology. Still, they do exist.

Multimedia technology has benefitted both the private and public sectors. For example, take the multimedia welfare program used in Visalia, a small town in the central valley of California. Visalia had a big problem. Because it had one of the highest rates of unemployment in the United States, the Visalia Office of Public Services had to process mounds of welfare paperwork for about 30 percent of the population. Handling all this paperwork was causing major difficulties. Before the Tulare Touch system was developed and implemented, errors in processing were costing the welfare office millions of dollars in lost time and extra personnel.

The Tulare Touch is a multimedia kiosk system used in Visalia to help people apply for public assistance. *Kiosks* are self-contained multimedia platforms used in remote locations where company personnel may not be around to answer questions or to gather information. With the Tulare Touch system, welfare recipients can enter their data themselves using a kiosk, cutting down the amount of time caseworkers need to work with customers, and reducing errors in the processing system. Using this system saves Tulare county over $20 million a year. Success stories such as this happen with more regularity as companies find ways for multimedia to deal with difficult business challenges.

The biggest challenge now is how to make multimedia technologies cost-effective for the general public. Despite many technological advances, the general price of sophisticated multimedia equipment is still far too expensive for most folks, and in many cases beyond the reach of most schools. It's hard to justify spending $600 to $3,500 or more on multimedia hardware when many schools still have to fight just to get money for $600 worth of text books. Still, given the consumer electronics market's ability to mass-produce sophisticated electronic equipment, it's just a matter of time before the price of multimedia systems becomes reasonable for both schools and for the home.

Multimedia in Business

Business is the one category of multimedia that is currently flourishing. As competition increases, it becomes even more important to offer better services and provide timely information to your clients. Multimedia technology offers today's businesses several ways to maintain a competitive edge, especially in marketing, public relations, and training.

Sales presentations

The interactive nature of multimedia brings spontaneity back into business presentations. Instead of hoping your video or slide show goes over with clients, you can use multimedia to customize the presentation. If your clients interrupt you because they don't want to hear about your manufacturing plans, but want financial data, no problem—just click to the financial section of your presentation. The accessibility of the information in your multimedia sales pitch makes it easy to conform the selling points within your presentation to the concerns of your clients.

Multimedia databases

Many businesses are already creating more powerful databases that can store and distribute digital media as easily as text. These powerful databases of the future will enable you to access any type of media from your desktop. The main data is in a central database server and it is distributed across a superfast data network throughout a company. This data could be anything from an interactive presentation on how your company health plan works, to animated computer data that shows a project in process.

Public kiosks

Generally a kiosk contains some type of computer, a computer monitor, and a touch screen. The *touch screen* allows people to control on-screen buttons by just pressing a section of the screen. Kiosks can provide information about a company or service as well as collect data from potential clients.

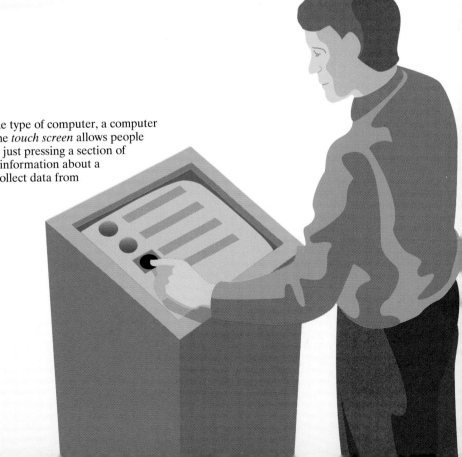

Multimedia in Education

It is crucial to understand that teachers will always be an integral part of multimedia education. Many have heralded the death of education due to multimedia technology. In fact, multimedia just enhances standard educational techniques. One good teacher is still worth more than any amount of hardware, no matter how sophisticated the technology. Multimedia in education

In-class presentations

With a large-screen projector and a multimedia playback system, teachers can use multimedia titles as a way to enhance their standard lesson plan and stimulate questions. The interactive nature of a multi-media title makes it much easier for a teacher to respond to student questions with graphic answers.

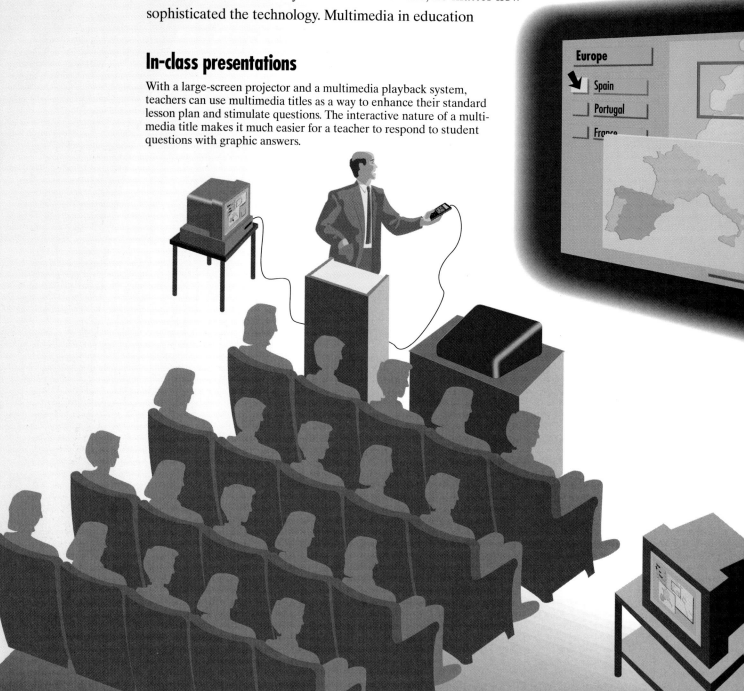

provides a new way for teachers to encourage one of the most rare and important elements of learning: curiosity. By taking one topic and adding as much related information as possible with graphics, text, video, and so on, a multimedia title allows teachers and students to explore topics from broader perspectives. When students uncover that key piece of information among the various multimedia titles, it can help them grasp difficult subjects by putting everything into perspective.

Home study

Students will be able to further explore topics at home using a standard multimedia platform. It will be possible to give assignments that require students to make their own interpretation of the facts as represented in the multimedia title. However, this two-way approach will depend upon the compatibility between the hardware used in school and in the home, as well as the complexity of the software in the multimedia title.

Multimedia in the Home

If you hear multimedia developers talk about the consumer electronics market with an almost reverent gleam in their eye, it's because many developers feel that the home market is where the big money is in multimedia. Most of this speculation is based on the success of home video games, which over the years have become a $3.5 billion industry. However, only time will tell in what shape multimedia technology may finally enter the home. After several failed attempts, developers learned that the general public is much more demanding when it comes to buying into new entertainment technology.

Low-cost home system

The low-priced home multimedia system will be a variation on one of the home video game systems, more than likely using some type of CD-ROM player that is hooked directly into a television.

High-end home system

Eventually, the high-end home system may look something like this. Instead of a regular video screen, an *HDTV* (High Definition Television) monitor is the main system display, offering greater image resolution and a wide screen aspect ratio. Services like home shopping and *video-on-demand* (where the cable company plays the movie you want to see when you want to see it) are easily integrated into the HDTV system.

CHAPTER

How a Multimedia Title Is Created

CREATING A MULTIMEDIA title is much like making a movie—it's a group effort that takes a lot of time and money. On some multimedia projects you'll find 20 or more people working on different facets of the project, each with a variety of titles and responsibilities within the production. It's not uncommon to find a producer who also writes the script or the music, and assists in graphic production. More often than not, being versatile is a matter of practicality, because personnel costs are nearly always the most expensive line items on any multimedia project. However, a multimedia production offers a creative individual considerable freedom when compared to the Hollywood studio scene. Where these people fit into the project depends upon whether they are involved in the design, production, or distribution portion of the process.

During the design stage, the production team has to make some hard decisions regarding the market they are targeting (such as home entertainment or computer reference), the platform they are developing for (Mac, Windows, Nintendo, and so on), the type of experience they want the user to have, and how they can make the most of their budget. These points are especially important because they will affect many areas during production, from the art design to the amount of digital video or animation in the project.

Multimedia developers work with production budgets that are radically lower than budgets for making movies. Today it costs anywhere from $3 million to over $100 million for a Hollywood studio to produce a movie for theatrical distribution, while it is rare for a multimedia title to cost more than a million dollars. That's not to say that multimedia titles are cheap to produce; in fact, most high-end commercial titles cost anywhere from $275,000 to $400,000.

During distribution, the multimedia title is transferred from a costly hard disk to more durable (and less expensive) media, such as CD-ROM, a floppy disk, or a video game cartridge. CD-ROMs are especially cost effective. After the $1,800 to $2,000 it costs to create your glass master disc, each copy of your CD-ROM costs only about one dollar.

The addition of a programmer to the production process constitutes another big difference between movies and multimedia. The programmer adds the essential interactivity between all of the media elements in the authoring program. Remember, interactivity prevents a multimedia title from being just a fancy slide presentation with sound and video. A good programmer also designs titles that can be modified to play on different platforms. This helps the production expand its distribution options.

Multimedia Design

During the initial design phase, all aspects of the multimedia project are carefully planned before production gets started. This is the stage where those heading up the title—the producer, the supervising art director, the interface designer, the content designer, and the main programmer—have to make decisions on key elements of the production.

Flow chart

One of the main tools used to organize everything during the design process is a *flow chart*, which is a map that shows how all of the elements in the title are connected. The flow chart serves as a blueprint that every member of the production team, from programmers to artists, will refer to during the production stage of the project.

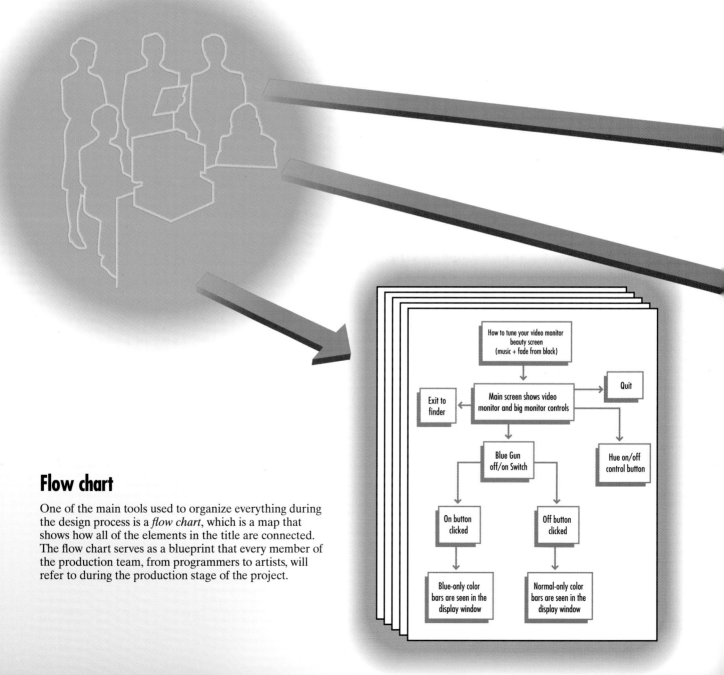

How to tune your video monitor
beauty screen
(music + fade from black)

Quit

Exit to finder

Main screen shows video monitor and big monitor controls

Blue Gun off/on Switch

Hue on/off control button

On button clicked

Off button clicked

Blue-only color bars are seen in the display window

Normal-only color bars are seen in the display window

How to correctly adjust the color on your video monitor script

B14. A properly adjusted monitor is crititcal in any desktop video application, especially in animation and videographic design.

To see how you use color bars to do this, just click on the wooden panel under the video monitor.

B15. While not all the controls you would find on a good video monitor are represented here, these are pretty much the main ones you need to use to properly adjust the monitors colors.

Click on the control panel.

B16. The blue gun simply turns off the red and green electron guns in the monitor, so that only a blue image is shown. This is a key

Script

Just like a movie, a multimedia title needs a *script* to keep track of the elements in the show. The script works in conjunction with the flow chart to provide a printed version of all the text, graphics, and dialogue used in the production.

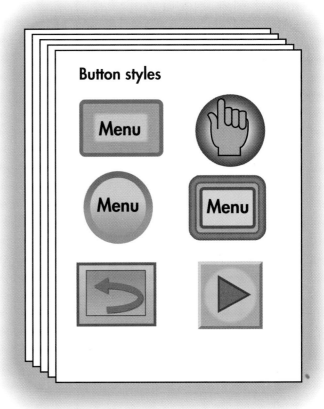

Button styles

Art proofs

During this time, the graphic artist and interface designer will create rough sketches or *proofs* of different interface and art elements for approval. This helps all of the members of the production team agree on the direction and focus of the title prior to production.

Multimedia Production

Production is the process of creating the media elements in a project, including sound, graphics, animation, and digital video. Often different members of the production team work on these elements simultaneously—while the art department creates and adjusts the graphics, the audio production team records the music and sound effects, and so on.

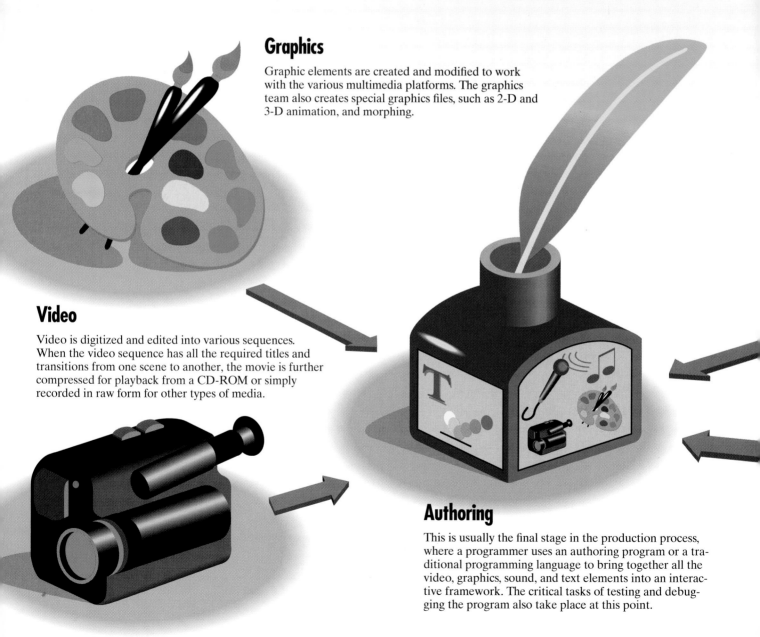

Graphics

Graphic elements are created and modified to work with the various multimedia platforms. The graphics team also creates special graphics files, such as 2-D and 3-D animation, and morphing.

Video

Video is digitized and edited into various sequences. When the video sequence has all the required titles and transitions from one scene to another, the movie is further compressed for playback from a CD-ROM or simply recorded in raw form for other types of media.

Authoring

This is usually the final stage in the production process, where a programmer uses an authoring program or a traditional programming language to bring together all the video, graphics, sound, and text elements into an interactive framework. The critical tasks of testing and debugging the program also take place at this point.

PRODUCTION NOTE One of the most important production tasks is the constant testing that occurs within each of the media groups. This is especially true when creating titles for CD-ROM because a CD-ROM drive can only transfer data to and from the computer at a fraction of the speed of a regular hard disk. This means that media elements, such as digital video and audio, must be optimized and compressed so they play back smoothly while not exceeding the CD-ROM's data transfer rate.

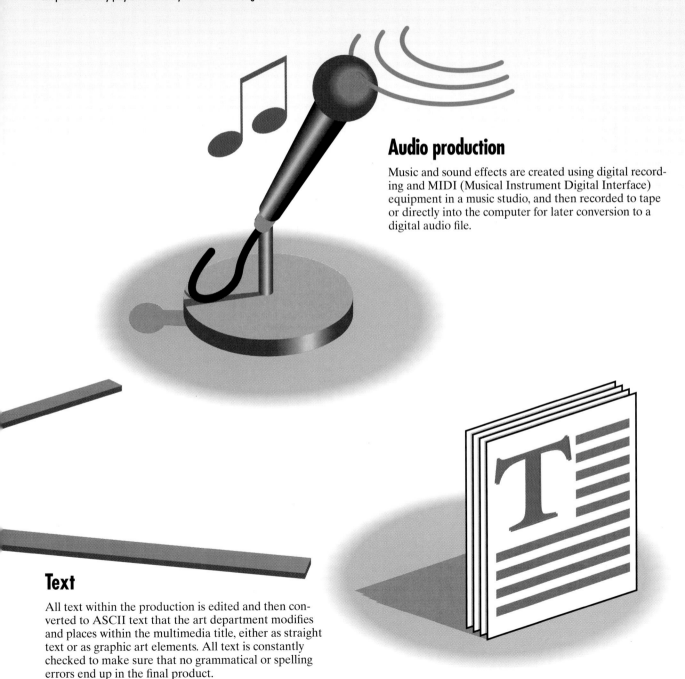

Audio production

Music and sound effects are created using digital recording and MIDI (Musical Instrument Digital Interface) equipment in a music studio, and then recorded to tape or directly into the computer for later conversion to a digital audio file.

Text

All text within the production is edited and then converted to ASCII text that the art department modifies and places within the multimedia title, either as straight text or as graphic art elements. All text is constantly checked to make sure that no grammatical or spelling errors end up in the final product.

Multimedia Distribution

Creating multimedia titles for various platforms is one of the biggest challenges that multimedia producers must face today. As you can see, there are many choices available when it comes to distributing a multimedia title, each of which has pros and cons. The bottom line: To increase the potential success of the project, a multimedia title needs to be available on as many platforms as possible. While different platforms are currently incompatible with each other, eventually this problem will get better. However, right now, accommodating the different platforms is similar to reshooting a movie for every brand of film projector.

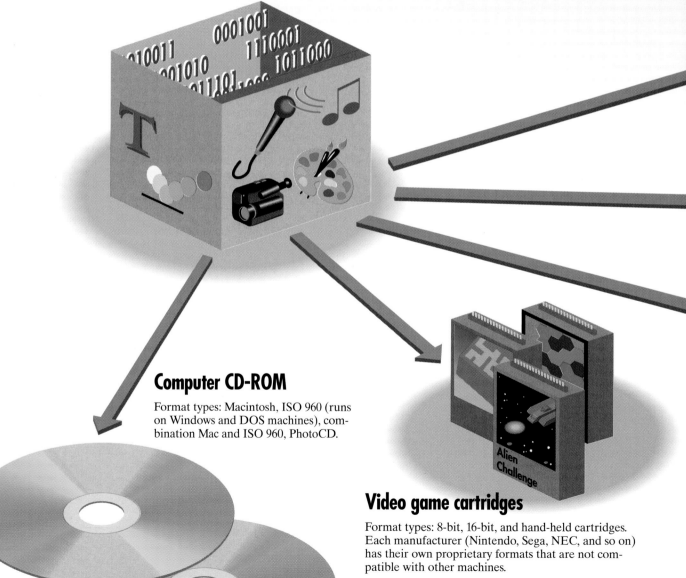

Computer CD-ROM

Format types: Macintosh, ISO 960 (runs on Windows and DOS machines), combination Mac and ISO 960, PhotoCD.

Video game cartridges

Format types: 8-bit, 16-bit, and hand-held cartridges. Each manufacturer (Nintendo, Sega, NEC, and so on) has their own proprietary formats that are not compatible with other machines.

Video game CD-ROM

Format types: 3DO, Sega Genesis CD, Super Nintendo CD, NEC Turbo Graphics CD, Phillips CD-I. Each manufacturer has their own proprietary formats that are not compatible with other machines.

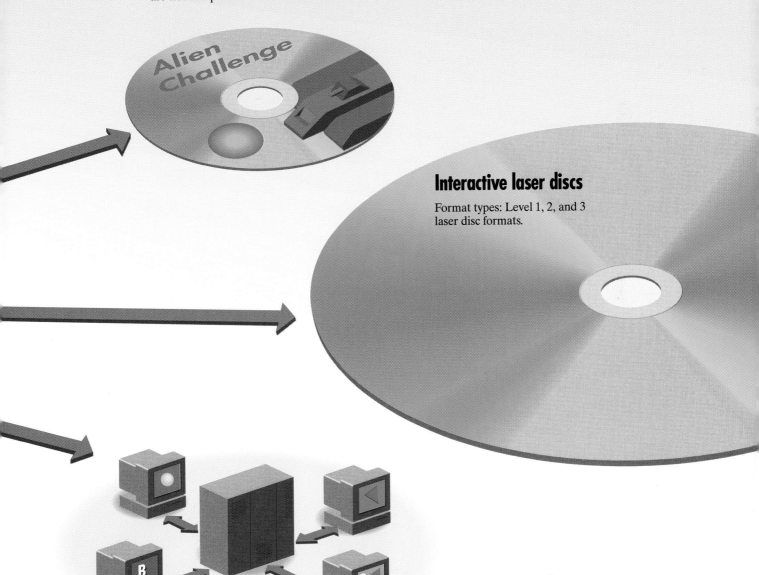

Interactive laser discs

Format types: Level 1, 2, and 3 laser disc formats.

Multimedia network

This is not a platform yet. However, networked multimedia is the backbone on which many new types of distribution, including interactive television, will be based.

MULTIMEDIA SYSTEM SOFTWARE AND HARDWARE

CONTENTS

YOU MAY FIND THIS surprising, but multimedia has been around for a while—more than a decade. Over ten years ago, you could combine sound, video, and so on, but you needed to hire a programmer to write a custom program for your system. This was the equivalent of paying an elite team thousands of dollars to press a record of your favorite songs, whereas now you would just record those songs onto a cassette tape. Until recently, only big business could afford the monstrous costs involved in producing multimedia programs. Today development tools are more user-friendly, and when they are combined with sophisticated system software and improvements in personal computer hardware technology, it is much easier and more cost-effective to create multimedia titles. Ten years ago, major corporations would have needed to spend over $100,000 to duplicate what a $600 multimedia author software program can do today. (Authoring programs are covered in Chapter 3.)

However, while multimedia may contain elements of films, video, magazines, and books, it lacks a crucial element that gives those media a much wider audience: standardization. The standard format for motion pictures in this country is 35mm film running at 24 frames per second, so a film that conforms to this standard can be shown in just about any film theater in the United States. Any television set that conforms to the National Television Standards Committee (NTSC) standard can show color video. Text in magazines and books is generally printed from left to right and top to bottom, with the exception of foreign language publications that conform to different rules of readability. Yet, the many brands of personal computers don't really have a standard way for dealing with things like showing graphics or playing sounds, so a multimedia program that worked on my computer had a good chance of not working on yours.

This section talks about some of the important developments in multimedia software and hardware standards. These developments have significantly improved the quality, variety, and market potential of multimedia titles. While the ongoing development of new technology will always stymie the creation of standards, at least there are a few in place today that help producers and distributors as they develop new multimedia products.

Standards will probably always be one of the most important issues in multimedia. Without standards it is doubtful that multimedia will ultimately succeed, any more than the videotape rental industry would exist if it had to keep 15 different formats of the same movie in stock.

CHAPTER 3

Authoring Programs

N THE PAST, MULTIMEDIA presentations required the services of a professional programmer. However, the current generation of authoring software makes it possible for nonprogrammers to create some fairly sophisticated multimedia titles that can play back sound, show movies, and move to different parts of the presentation when you click on a button. One of the first authoring tools that was generally accessible to nonprogrammers was Apple's HyperCard. Once you learned how to use HyperTalk, the basic programming language of HyperCard, you could create presentations that did everything from play back simple animations, to trigger external devices (such as a laser disc player). Today, software tools such as Macromind Director, Authorware, and Toolbook make authoring even more powerful.

Yet the ease of creating programs with these tools is too often matched by a reduction in performance speed, because these authoring programs are interpreted programming languages. Unlike a compiled computer program, which communicates directly with binary code, an *interpreted language* has to translate commands into binary computer code from within another program. To speed up this procedure, programs such as HyperCard and Macromind Director began to incorporate small pieces of binary computer code in the authoring package to speed up some commands or add special functions. These pieces of code are sometimes called *Xobjects* or *Xcommands*—the *X* standing for any variable name. For instance, to speed up an animation, you might use an Xcommand that would load all of the animation into memory automatically, while you might use an Xobject to trigger an audio CD player to play music when the user clicks on an on-screen musical note. Although these Xcommands and Xobjects can add speed and functionality to a program, the limitations of the interpreted programming language itself still put a drag on the title's performance.

So, in keeping with the proverb that everything old is new again, traditional programming has once again been adopted as the standard aproach for developing professional multimedia titles, as producers constantly struggle to improve the quality and performance of their titles.

How Authoring Programs Work

1 The first step in using an authoring program is to import all the media elements used in your title. While some programs can create animation and graphics from within the program, generally most developers use a variety of graphic, audio, video, and animation tools when creating a title. Consequently, most authoring programs can import many types of media file formats, from the bitmapped graphics of a Macintosh PICT file, to a Windows .WAV sound file.

2 Once you've added all graphics, text, audio, animation, and digital video into the program, you can assign different relationships and actions to each element by adding interactive control. This could be as simple as having a sound play when you click on one part of the screen, to setting up a series of animations and sounds that play when you click a button on-screen.

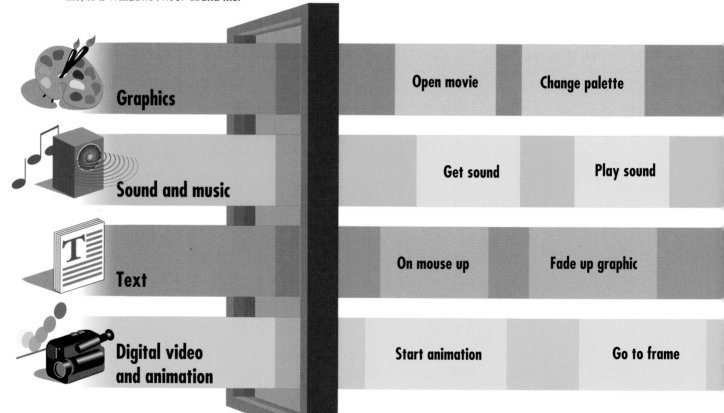

Graphics

Sound and music

Text

Digital video and animation

Open movie	Change palette
Get sound	Play sound
On mouse up	Fade up graphic
Start animation	Go to frame

3 When you run the program, the interpreter part of the authoring program takes all the commands and relationships that you have defined in the authoring interface, and converts these commands into a binary code that your computer's operating system can understand. The converted program is then sent to the central processing unit (CPU) on your machine, which sends out orders to your system to play back any audio; display all text, video, and animation; and trigger any external devices.

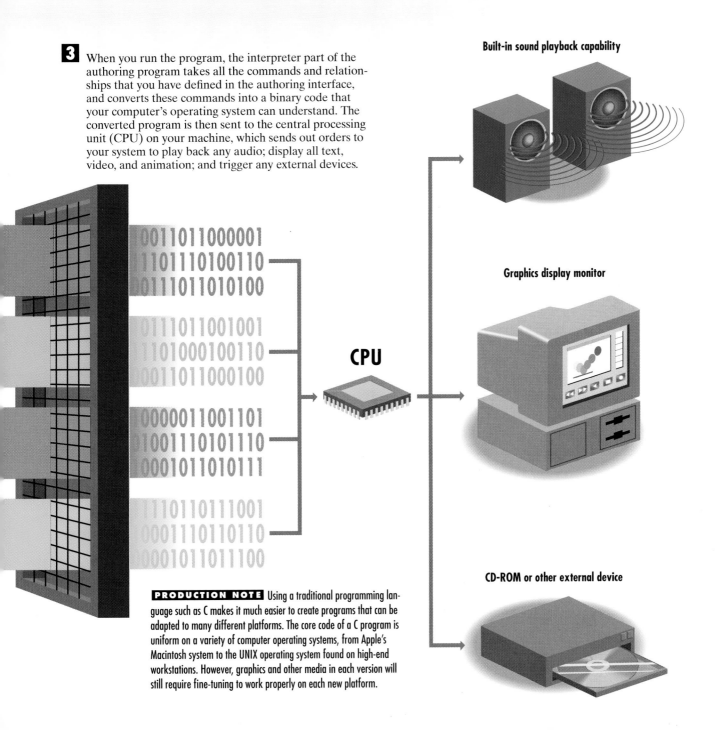

Built-in sound playback capability

Graphics display monitor

CPU

CD-ROM or other external device

PRODUCTION NOTE Using a traditional programming language such as C makes it much easier to create programs that can be adapted to many different platforms. The core code of a C program is uniform on a variety of computer operating systems, from Apple's Macintosh system to the UNIX operating system found on high-end workstations. However, graphics and other media in each version will still require fine-tuning to work properly on each new platform.

How ScriptX Works

Developed as a joint venture between Apple and IBM, ScriptX from Kaleida Labs is an object-oriented scripting language that offers a unique solution to the problem of multimedia distribution. Unlike traditional programming, *object-oriented programming* (OOP) uses modular, premade pieces of code or *objects* to create a program. Instead of working on a hardware standard, ScriptX is a software standard that is independent of any hardware platform. This means that a multimedia program developed on a Macintosh or PC computer and saved as a ScriptX document can play back on any computer or multimedia device that supports a ScriptX playback or "runtime" environment.

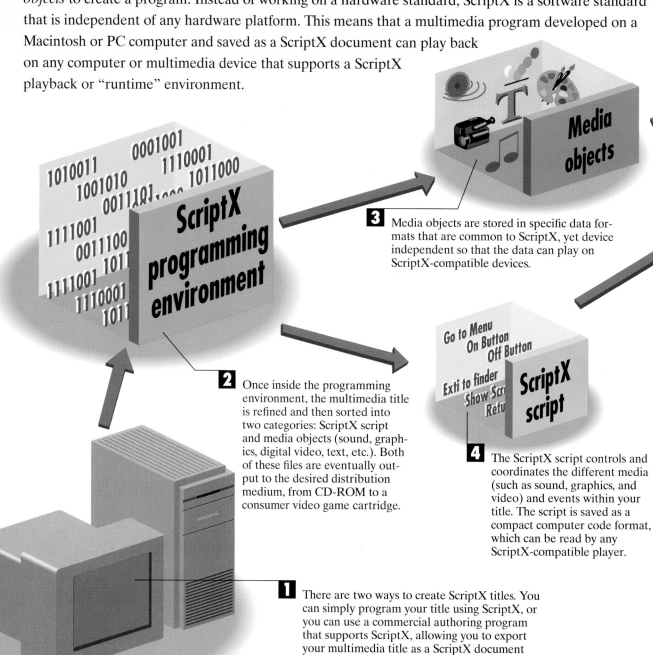

3 Media objects are stored in specific data formats that are common to ScriptX, yet device independent so that the data can play on ScriptX-compatible devices.

2 Once inside the programming environment, the multimedia title is refined and then sorted into two categories: ScriptX script and media objects (sound, graphics, digital video, text, etc.). Both of these files are eventually output to the desired distribution medium, from CD-ROM to a consumer video game cartridge.

4 The ScriptX script controls and coordinates the different media (such as sound, graphics, and video) and events within your title. The script is saved as a compact computer code format, which can be read by any ScriptX-compatible player.

1 There are two ways to create ScriptX titles. You can simply program your title using ScriptX, or you can use a commercial authoring program that supports ScriptX, allowing you to export your multimedia title as a ScriptX document from within your favorite authoring program.

5 When played back from the distribution medium, the ScriptX script and media objects are sent through the ScriptX Runtime environment of your playback device. ScriptX adjusts the playback and response of certain media as necessary to keep the performance of the title on the playback machine consistent with what was originally created on the development platform.

PRODUCTION NOTE One of the advantages of using ScriptX is that all the basic capabilities needed to create multimedia content—such as digital video and audio, animation control, search and retrieval commands—are built into ScriptX as objects that you can easily customize and reuse. For example, if you create an object that can measure from one point on the screen to another, you could use the core programming of this object to create a ruler in a program on graphic design or an on-screen distance odometer in a title on geography. By using object-oriented programming tools, developers can build up large libraries of objects that they can quickly apply to different projects.

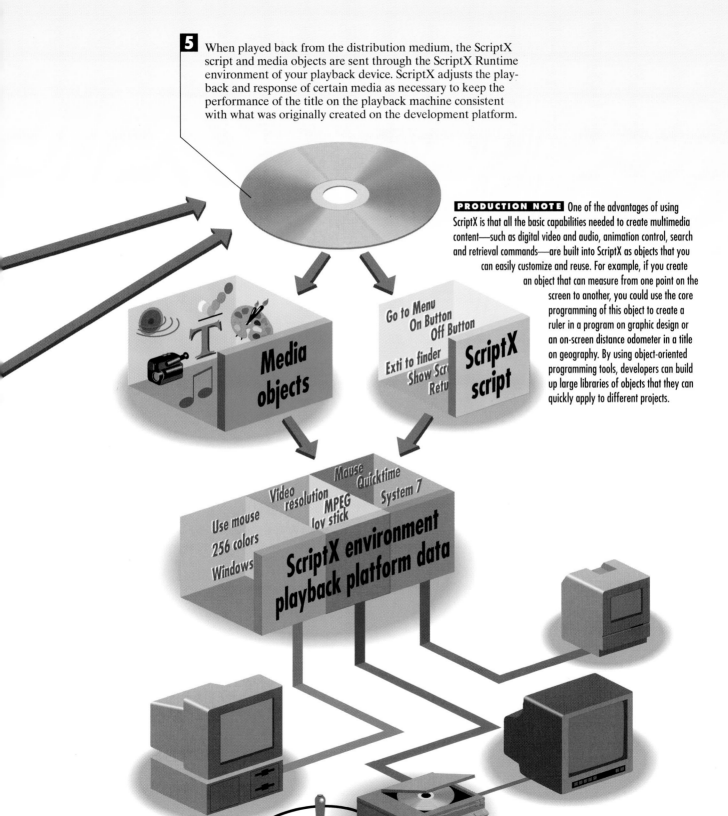

Media objects

Go to Menu
On Button
Off Button
Exti to finder
Show Scr
Retu

ScriptX script

Mouse
Quicktime
Video
resolution   System 7
MPEG
Joy stick
Use mouse
256 colors
Windows
ScriptX environment playback platform data

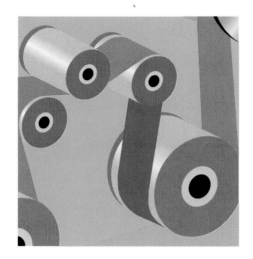

Multimedia Extensions in Windows

BM PCS AND compatibles have had a hard time with multimedia. While the many models and vendors in the market make Windows and DOS PCs the most cost-effective personal computers available, the variety of standard hardware and system software makes it difficult to play multimedia titles. The reverse is true for Macintosh computers, which kept everything proprietary, making it easy to keep hardware and software consistent—and making Macs more expensive than comparable PC systems.

In an attempt to apply to all PCs the same type of standards that Macs have enjoyed for years, Microsoft Corporation developed the Multimedia extensions for their ubiquitous Windows operating system software. The Multimedia extensions within Windows add several multimedia capabilities to the Windows OS, including *RIFF (Resource Interchange File Format)*, a standard file format for multimedia data, including bitmapped graphics, animation, digital audio, and MIDI (Musical Instrument Digital Interface) files; digital audio playback and recording capabilities; *Media Control Interface (MCI)* software, which enables Windows machines to control external devices, such as CD-ROMs, VCRs, and laser disc players; the ability to play MIDI files from different programs; and several utilities—the Sound Recorder, the Media Player, and the MIDI mapper—which act as either controls or filters for digital audio, device controls, or MIDI data.

The Multimedia extensions do not currently provide a way to play back digital video. Microsoft's Video for Windows or *AVI (Audio Video Interleave)* software, and Apple's QuickTime for Windows software are available as add-ons to the extensions. These add-ons help your computer play back and synchronize digital video and audio.

Development efforts with Windows-based PCs are under way to improve graphics capability for multimedia playback. Most standard Windows graphics are limited to 256 colors, unless you install a custom software and graphics card. A 24-bit driver that will enable your system to display over 16 million colors on screen is in the works as a built-in feature for Windows.

How Windows Multimedia Extensions Work

You won't see much of the software in the Multimedia extensions because it operates in the background most of the time. The MIDI Mapper, Sound Recorder, and Media Player utilities are the direct interface to the different software sections within the Multimedia extensions in Windows.

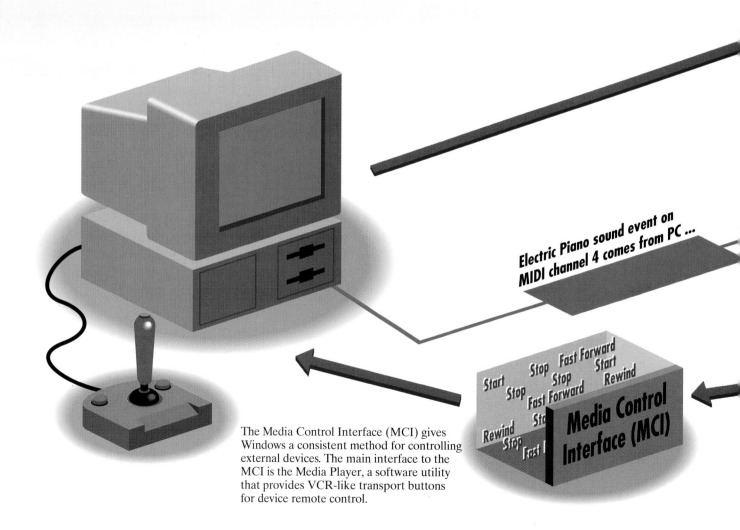

Electric Piano sound event on MIDI channel 4 comes from PC ...

The Media Control Interface (MCI) gives Windows a consistent method for controlling external devices. The main interface to the MCI is the Media Player, a software utility that provides VCR-like transport buttons for device remote control.

Media Control Interface (MCI)

Start Stop Fast Forward Start
Stop Stop Rewind
Fast Forward
Rewind Stop
Stop Fast F

When used with a third-party sound card, the Sound Recorder utility allows you to play back and record digital audio straight into your PC as .WAV sound files. Like the Media Player, the Sound Recorder software accesses and controls the sound hardware using a transport control to start, stop, and record digital audio.

The MIDI Mapper helps you make sure the events that are specified in the MIDI file are sent to the correct MIDI instrument. For example, let's say a series of chords for an electric piano instrument is output from your computer as MIDI channel 4. If your electric piano sound is actually preset to MIDI channel 9 on your synthesizer, you can use the MIDI Mapper software to redirect the data to the right location.

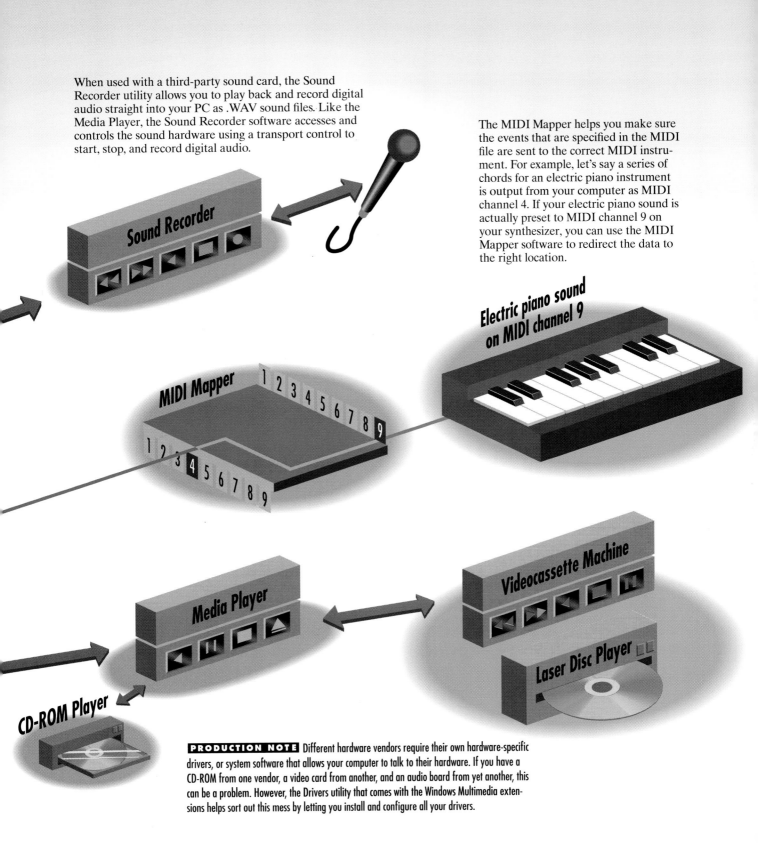

PRODUCTION NOTE Different hardware vendors require their own hardware-specific drivers, or system software that allows your computer to talk to their hardware. If you have a CD-ROM from one vendor, a video card from another, and an audio board from yet another, this can be a problem. However, the Drivers utility that comes with the Windows Multimedia extensions helps sort out this mess by letting you install and configure all your drivers.

How Video for Windows Works

The Video for Windows software is an extra set of programs that add digital video playback and editing capabilities to the Multimedia extensions for Windows. This addition to the Multimedia extensions brings digital video functionality to the hundreds of thousands of Windows machines out on the market today. You can play Video for Windows movies from any Windows application that supports Windows 3.1. While Video for Windows is a separate package from the Multimedia extensions, it is probable that Microsoft will bundle it as one package to stay competitive with Apple's QuickTime software, which combines similar functions into one software package.

PRODUCTION NOTE It's interesting to note that while Apple is creating a Windows version of its QuickTime software, Microsoft is working on a Mac version of Video for Windows. The driving force behind both of these ventures is to expand the playability of multimedia titles beyond the original development platform.

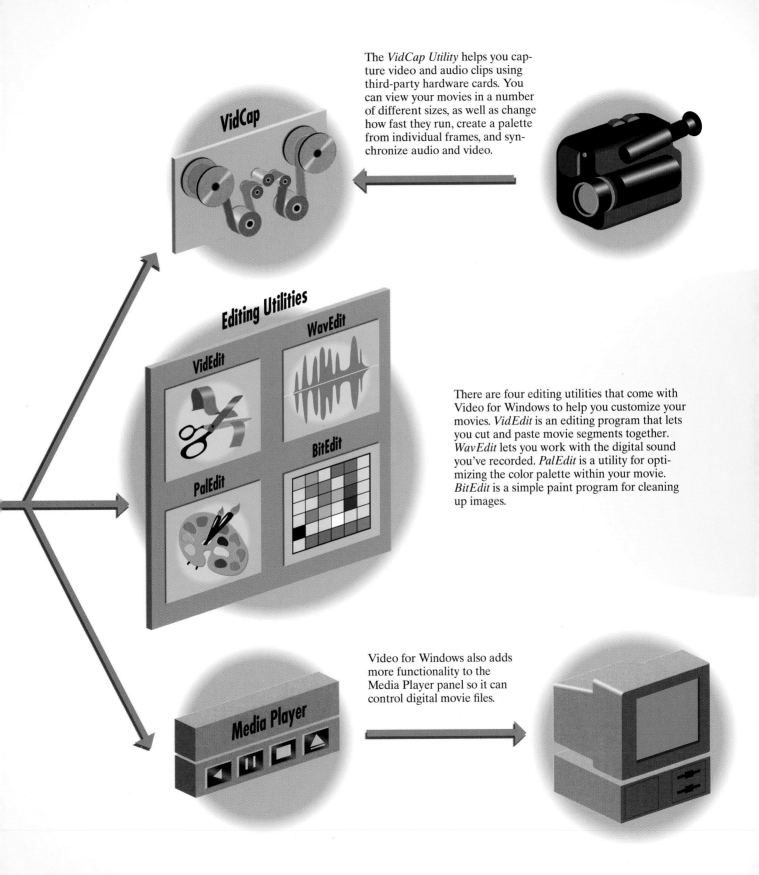

The *VidCap Utility* helps you capture video and audio clips using third-party hardware cards. You can view your movies in a number of different sizes, as well as change how fast they run, create a palette from individual frames, and synchronize audio and video.

There are four editing utilities that come with Video for Windows to help you customize your movies. *VidEdit* is an editing program that lets you cut and paste movie segments together. *WavEdit* lets you work with the digital sound you've recorded. *PalEdit* is a utility for optimizing the color palette within your movie. *BitEdit* is a simple paint program for cleaning up images.

Video for Windows also adds more functionality to the Media Player panel so it can control digital movie files.

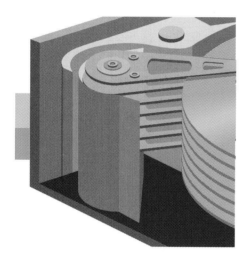

QuickTime

THERE ARE OVER a dozen graphics, sound, and animation formats in the personal computer industry. These varied formats are a problem for both multimedia developers and users who need standard file formats that can play on any standard hardware system. QuickTime is a system software extension that establishes a common file format that can fit different software and hardware applications. This capability makes QuickTime one of the most important breakthroughs for Macintosh-based multimedia. Third-party developers can add QuickTime's functionality to their hardware and software, making QuickTime compatible with a variety of applications for graphics, animation, sound, and so on.

Most people think of QuickTime as software that plays video on the Macintosh desktop. Actually, it's best to think of QuickTime as an expandable suitcase for all kinds of digital media. Not only can you stuff large digital audio and video files into QuickTime, but you can also take that data with you from one application to another. Any QuickTime-compatible application, such as a multimedia title, a business presentation, or even a word processing application, can play video, sound, and animation from within its program.

Here's the other nice thing about QuickTime: It is an open-ended system. You'll be able to use QuickTime to take advantage of any new hardware or software technology that comes out over the next few years. QuickTime uses a special set of software routines in conjunction with custom third-party software to add new features and new technology onto its core code. Just drop a new compression scheme into the Extensions folder in your Mac's System Folder, and you're all set. This same interface applies to external video and audio digitizing hardware. Instead of trying to create software that fits every known manufacturer, Apple made QuickTime flexible enough to recognize custom code from hardware vendors, which lets you use that hardware from any QuickTime-compatible application.

While the QuickTime software cannot even begin to play full-screen, full-motion video without a lot of hardware, it is a great start toward bringing new types of media into new Mac applications.

How QuickTime Works in the Mac

The QuickTime software is divided into three main parts, which work unseen in the background while your application is running. Each part works in conjunction with the others, especially the Movie Toolbox and the Image Compression Manager, which both rely heavily on the various compression algorithms accessed from the Component Manager.

1 The *Movie Toolbox* contains several additions to the Mac system software that third-party developers can add to their applications. For example, the Movie Toolbox specifies a file format for keeping sound synchronized in digital movies, provides routines for cutting and pasting QuickTime movies, offers a standard interface for playing or manipulating movies, and even adds a Preview window to the standard Mac Open dialog box.

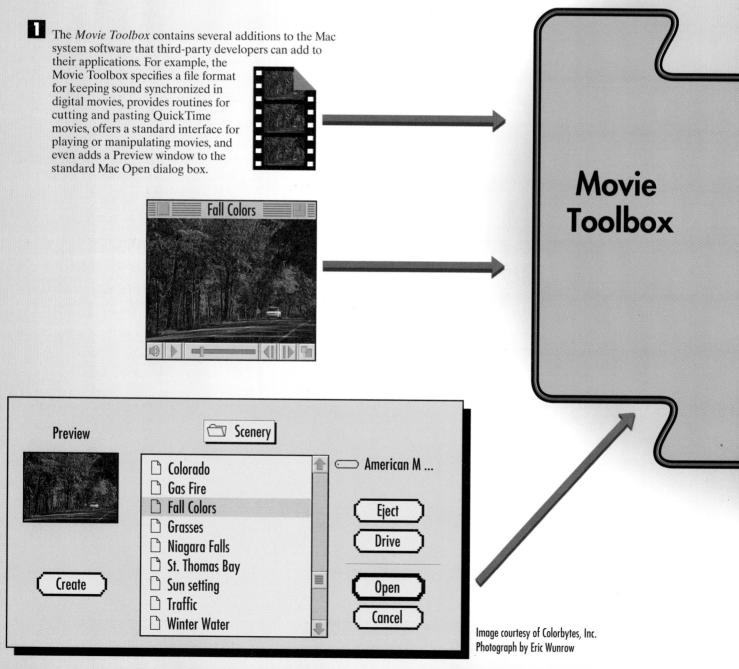

Image courtesy of Colorbytes, Inc.
Photograph by Eric Wunrow

2 The *Component Manager* keeps track of all the custom software
add-ons that are in the System Folder when you start up your
Mac. Instead of having to remake hardware to fit QuickTime,
third-party developers just create a small component (called a
VDIG, or *video digitizer component*) specifically for their hardware device. This enables you to use any third-party hardware
within any QuickTime application, regardless of the original
manufacturer.

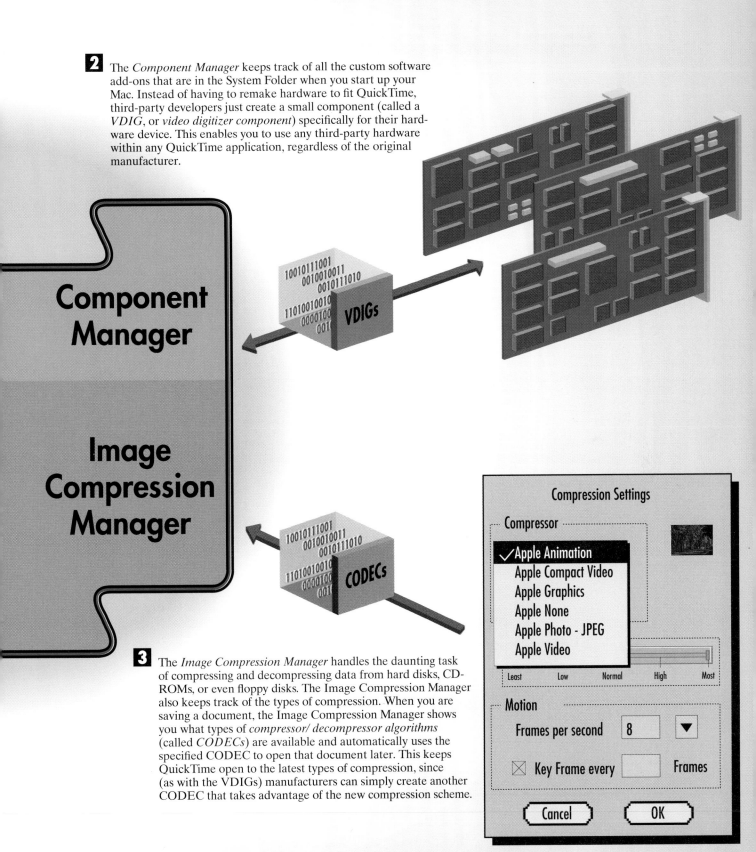

Component Manager

Image Compression Manager

Compression Settings

┌─ Compressor ──────────────────────
│ ✓ Apple Animation
│   Apple Compact Video
│   Apple Graphics
│   Apple None
│   Apple Photo - JPEG
│   Apple Video

Least   Low   Normal   High   Most

┌─ Motion ──────────────────────
│ Frames per second   8   ▼
│
│ ☒ Key Frame every [   ] Frames

(Cancel)   (OK)

3 The *Image Compression Manager* handles the daunting task
of compressing and decompressing data from hard disks, CD-
ROMs, or even floppy disks. The Image Compression Manager
also keeps track of the types of compression. When you are
saving a document, the Image Compression Manager shows
you what types of *compressor/ decompressor algorithms*
(called *CODECs*) are available and automatically uses the
specified CODEC to open that document later. This keeps
QuickTime open to the latest types of compression, since
(as with the VDIGs) manufacturers can simply create another
CODEC that takes advantage of the new compression scheme.

How QuickTime CODECs Work

QuickTime has five main built-in CODECs for compressing and decompressing image files. Which one you use depends upon what kind of image you are using and what you want to do with it.

1 The Graphics and Photo/JPEG CODECs compress still images. The *Graphics* CODEC can compress standard Mac graphics that contain the standard 256 colors (also called 8-bit color). The *Photo/ JPEG* CODEC uses a unique form of compression called *JPEG* (*Joint Photographic Experts Group*), which provides the best compression possible for full-color photographs and art (for more on JPEG, see Chapter 14).

2 The *Animation* CODEC quickly compresses and decompresses computer animation files. While it compresses files using a system similar to the Graphics CODEC, the Animation CODEC is designed to display images much more quickly. Consequently, files compressed with the Animation CODEC are twice as large than if they were compressed individually with the Graphics CODEC.

3 The Apple Video and Compact Video CODECs are made for compressing video so you can play movie files on your Mac. The main difference between the two is in file compression and playback. The *Apple Video* CODEC compresses and decompresses images quickly, while the *Compact Video* CODEC takes more time to compress the image.

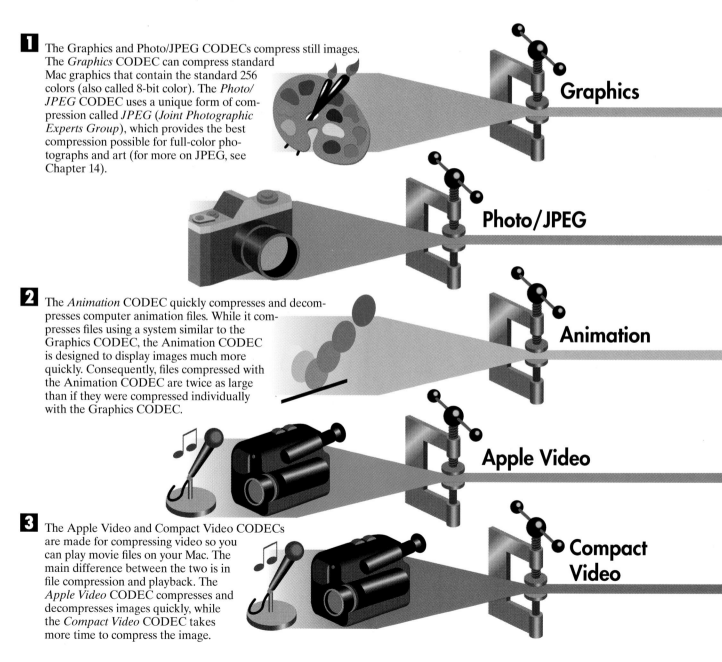

Graphics

Photo/JPEG

Animation

Apple Video

Compact Video

4 You can use both the graphics and animation compressors in any program that uses images within the application. For example, if you've saved an image in the Photo/JPEG format, you could open it in a page layout program. QuickTime automatically detects what kind of compression was used and works with the page layout program to display and later print the image.

5 Because both the Animation and the Apple Video CODEC do not reduce file sizes very much, for optimal performance you generally must play back these files from a hard disk, which has a much faster access time than other storage media. The compression formula used in the Compact Video CODEC was designed to distribute and play back QuickTime movies on CD-ROMs.

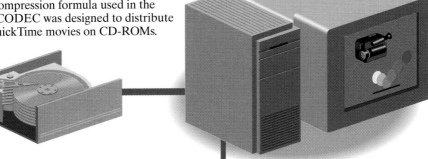

PRODUCTION NOTE The *Compact Video* (also called *CinePak*) CODEC is actually a form of *MPEG* (*Motion Picture Experts Group*) compression, which is being developed for many consumer electronic systems as a new way of distributing video (for more on MPEG see Chapter 14).

How Computer Multimedia Systems Work

COMPUTER-BASED MULTIMEDIA systems break down into two main categories: playback systems and authoring systems. *Playback systems* are personal computers that contain the minimum hardware and software necessary to play a multimedia title. Generally you will have to add hardware or software to a basic personal computer in order to turn it into a playback system. Adding a few pieces of system software and a CD-ROM drive will usually do the trick.

A Macintosh computer generally requires less additional hardware and software than a Windows or DOS computer in order to convert it into a playback system. This is because the Mac has long had many built-in capabilities that are now appearing in PCs, such as enhanced sound and graphics support. The Mac is a *closed system* for the most part, meaning only Apple can create Mac computers, which makes it easier for developers to recognize the standard requirements for Mac multimedia programs.

However, the *MPC* (*Multimedia Personal Computer*) standard has helped standardize hardware and software for multimedia on Windows and DOS computers. The MPC standard was developed several years ago; it set up a minimum requirement list to which any individual product or system should conform in order to be able to play back multimedia titles. While hardware conflicts in PC systems haven't stopped completely, the MPC standard cuts down on basic incompatibility problems between PC multimedia hardware.

Authoring systems are the computers and external hardware that multimedia developers use to create their multimedia titles. Because these machines need as much muscle as possible to perform many high-powered functions, an authoring system must be as powerful as a developer can afford—especially if the developer is adding digital audio or video to his or her projects.

You can spend just as much or as little as you want on a multimedia authoring system. This chapter shows standard setups that multimedia producers throughout the country use, but you can easily add or subtract hardware and software according to the type of title that you want to create. For example, if your title doesn't use sound, you won't need the audio digitizing cards or the audio editing software, which could deduct as much as $2,000 from the cost of your system. Also, if you plan to collaborate with other artists, composers, or animators, there is a good chance they would have any specific hardware or software you need.

How Mac Multimedia Systems Work

Minimum Playback System

Low-end Mac Model specifications: 16 MHz '030 central processing unit (CPU) (Mac LC II models and above), 4MB of RAM, a 40MB hard disk, a CD-ROM player, and a 13" color monitor. The software consists of System 6.08 or System 7.0x, and QuickTime 1.5 or higher.

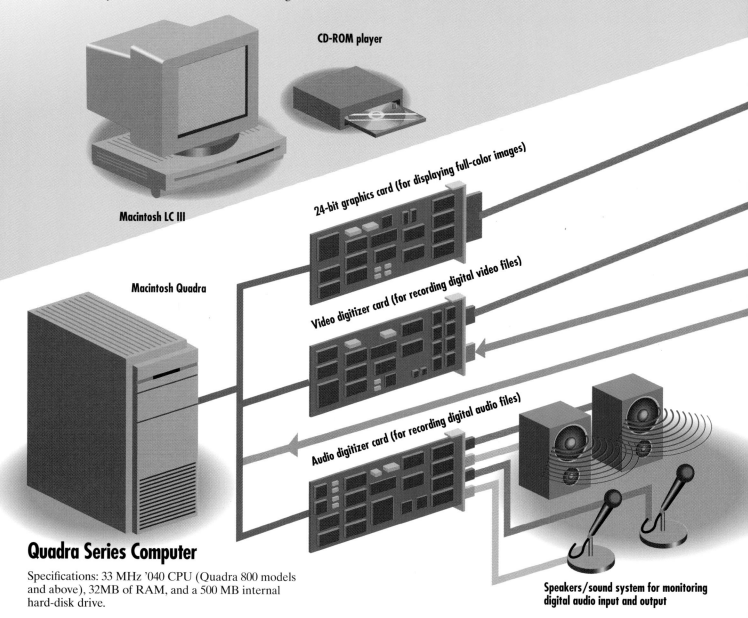

CD-ROM player

Macintosh LC III

24-bit graphics card (for displaying full-color images)

Macintosh Quadra

Video digitizer card (for recording digital video files)

Audio digitizer card (for recording digital audio files)

Quadra Series Computer

Specifications: 33 MHz '040 CPU (Quadra 800 models and above), 32MB of RAM, and a 500 MB internal hard-disk drive.

Speakers/sound system for monitoring digital audio input and output

Minimum Authoring System

Authoring systems on any platform vary widely in price, depending upon the complexity of the titles you are creating. The sky is the limit; after purchasing the fastest Mac possible, you can (and probably will) add thousands of dollars of external hardware.

A second monitor is often used to display graphics, the output of digital graphics cards, or (if a video monitor is used) to design graphics for use on video systems.

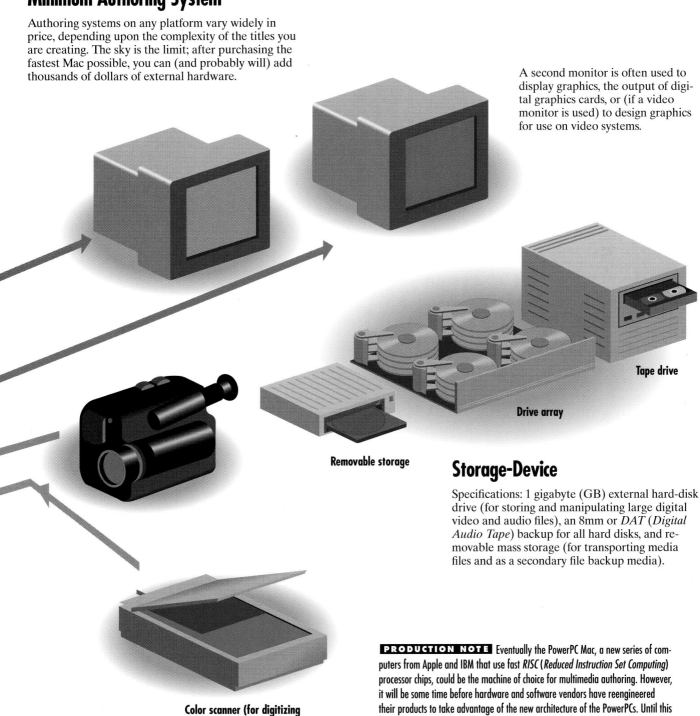

Tape drive

Drive array

Removable storage

Storage-Device

Specifications: 1 gigabyte (GB) external hard-disk drive (for storing and manipulating large digital video and audio files), an 8mm or *DAT* (*Digital Audio Tape*) backup for all hard disks, and removable mass storage (for transporting media files and as a secondary file backup media).

Color scanner (for digitizing photographs and line art)

PRODUCTION NOTE Eventually the PowerPC Mac, a new series of computers from Apple and IBM that use fast *RISC* (*Reduced Instruction Set Computing*) processor chips, could be the machine of choice for multimedia authoring. However, it will be some time before hardware and software vendors have reengineered their products to take advantage of the new architecture of the PowerPCs. Until this happens, the PowerPC will have to run current Mac software in an emulation mode, which will slow down the application speed dramatically.

How MPC Multimedia Systems Work

The minimum system shown here conforms to the MPC Level 2 specification, as most industry experts agreed that the original MPC Level 1 specification was not powerful enough to play back sophisticated multimedia titles. This playback environment is robust enough to smoothly play back animation, digital audio, and digital animation files.

MPC Level 2 Playback System

Specifications: a 25 MHz 486SX (or compatible) CPU, 4MB of RAM (8 recommended), and a 160MB or larger hard drive. CD-ROM drive: double speed (300K/sec sustained transfer rate), CD-ROM XA ready/multisession capable, and enhanced drivers for sophisticated audio support. Audio requires a 16-bit digital audio card, music synthesizer, and on-board analog mixing. Video requires a 640 × 480 screen (approx. 13") with at least 64K colors. I/O requires serial and parallel ports, a MIDI in/out port, and a joystick port. You will also need Windows 3.0 or higher.

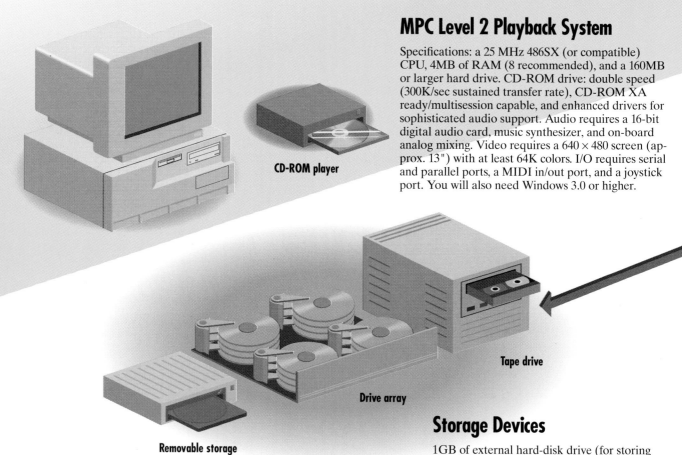

CD-ROM player

Tape drive

Drive array

Removable storage

Storage Devices

1GB of external hard-disk drive (for storing and manipulating large digital video and audio files), 8mm or DAT backup for all hard disks, and removable mass storage (for transporting media files and as a secondary file backup media).

Windows/DOS Authoring Systems

As on the Mac platform, a Windows or DOS authoring system will vary widely in price, although you can plan on spending thousands of dollars for external hardware.

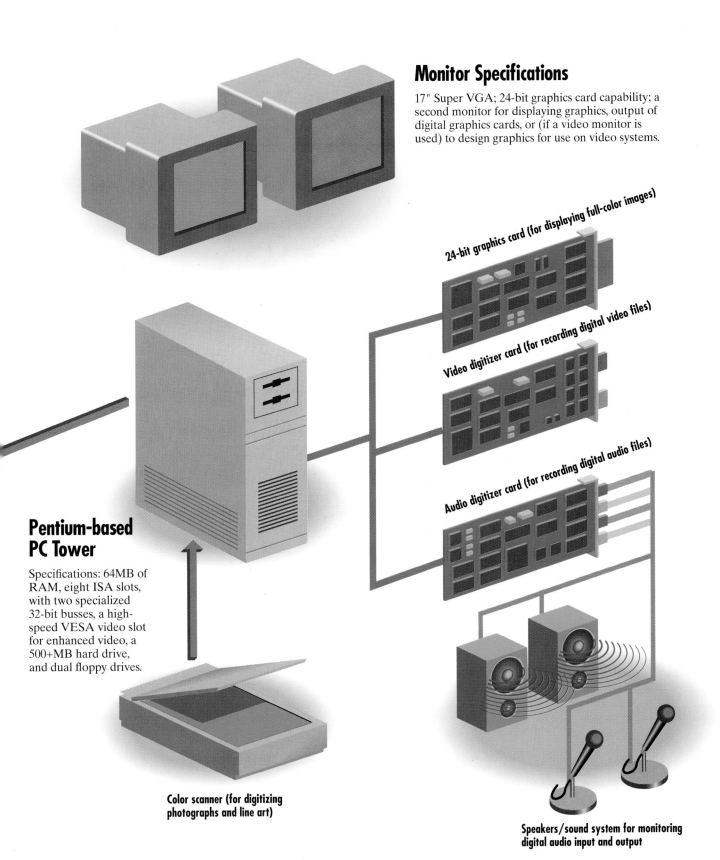

Monitor Specifications

17" Super VGA; 24-bit graphics card capability; a second monitor for displaying graphics, output of digital graphics cards, or (if a video monitor is used) to design graphics for use on video systems.

24-bit graphics card (for displaying full-color images)

Video digitizer card (for recording digital video files)

Audio digitizer card (for recording digital audio files)

Pentium-based PC Tower

Specifications: 64MB of RAM, eight ISA slots, with two specialized 32-bit busses, a high-speed VESA video slot for enhanced video, a 500+MB hard drive, and dual floppy drives.

Color scanner (for digitizing photographs and line art)

Speakers/sound system for monitoring digital audio input and output

How Mass Storage in Multimedia Works

YOU'RE PROBABLY ASKING why a book on multimedia includes a whole chapter on a topic as mundane as mass storage. Storage technologies aren't really as exciting as digital audio or video recording systems. Besides, the only kind of storage device that most users come into contact with is a CD-ROM or a video game cartridge, so why even bother to mention it?

Here's the reason: By using improved storage technology, producers can enhance the quality of digital video and audio media files and ultimately the complexity of the titles that you see. The digital audio and full-motion video files in multimedia titles contain huge amounts of data and put a tremendous strain on mass storage technology. The digital movie that you see in your favorite game title might look small to you, but it was a much larger digital video file before it was compressed and optimized for playback on a CD-ROM or video game cartridge.

Storage is a major concern during production, because two of the best features of multimedia—digital audio and video—are also the biggest storage hogs. A single minute of CD-quality stereo sound will fill up just over seven high-density floppy disks or 10 megabytes (MB) on a hard-disk drive. Digital video is even more demanding; just 25 minutes of full-screen digital video with good quality audio can fill up a 2 gigabyte (GB) hard disk.

Storage space isn't the only problem; to work properly, digital video and audio digitizer cards must quickly send tremendous amounts of data to and receive it from a hard disk when you record or play back audio or video. This also puts some severe limits on the type of drive that you can use for digital media production, because most drives send and receive data at less than half the volume required by some digital video editing systems.

The illustrations in this chapter depict several mass storage technologies that directly affect multimedia title creation. The illustrations also show how the technologies are used throughout the production cycle. These mundane storage technologies—drive arrays, magneto-optical disks, and tape backup systems—are some of the most important tools in multimedia production.

How Big Hard Disks and Drive Arrays Work in Multimedia

Not only do digital video and audio take up tremendous amounts of hard-disk space, but they also need drives that can send large amounts of data back and forth quickly to keep the audio and video playing and recording smoothly. Currently, magnetic disk drives are the only technology that can handle the demands of sophisticated digital audio and video production.

Hard Disks

Because of the high amounts of storage required for digital audio and video, as well as graphics, most multimedia producers invest in at least a single external hard-disk drive. Hard-disk drives offer speed (they can get to or access data very quickly); high data throughput (they can send large amounts of data to and from the computer); and plenty of storage space (most producers use drives that are 1GB or larger).

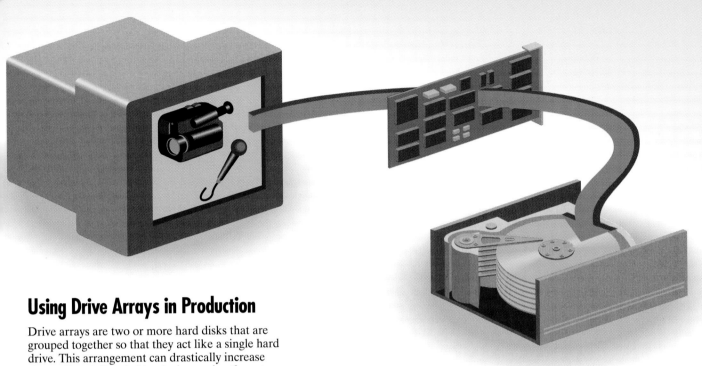

Using Drive Arrays in Production

Drive arrays are two or more hard disks that are grouped together so that they act like a single hard drive. This arrangement can drastically increase the quality of digital video by increasing the amount of data that you can record at one time.

When you record digital video, using higher quality settings causes the amount of compression to decrease and the amount of data that the digital video system needs to send and receive from the hard drive to increase. This problem is compounded when you record full-screen video images with some digital video systems, which can swamp even the fastest single hard drives with the amount of data that they send at one time.

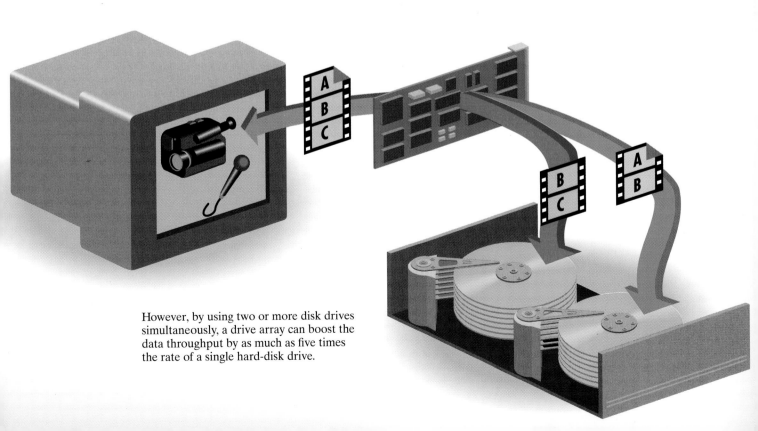

However, by using two or more disk drives simultaneously, a drive array can boost the data throughput by as much as five times the rate of a single hard-disk drive.

Using Magneto-Optical Drives in Multimedia

Magneto-optical (MO) technology is the most exciting development in multimedia mass storage, because magneto-optical disk media offer large amounts of storage in a durable package. As optical drive and optical media technology continue to develop, magneto-optical technology has expanded into archiving, transporting and recording video, audio, graphics, and animation files.

Archiving/Secondary Backup

While the cost per megabyte is higher than with DAT or 8mm tape, MO disks are also used to back up media files during and after a production. Unlike with most DAT or 8mm tape systems, you can read and access files on an MO disk in real time as though they were on a different hard disk.

Transporting Files

MO disks are great for transporting files from one office to another, even if the offices are across the country. MO disks aren't affected by shock or stray magnetic fields the way that hard drives, floppy disks, and tape backups are, so you can feel secure sending your precious production files via air or local courier.

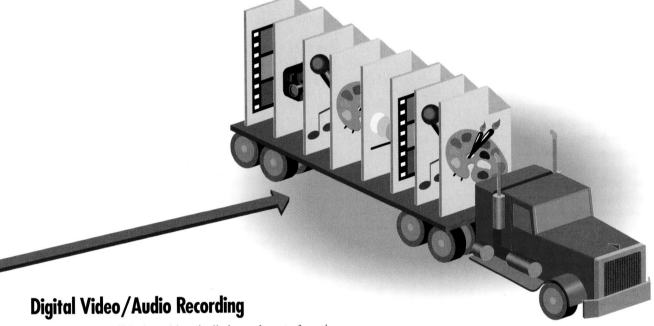

Digital Video/Audio Recording

Magneto-optical disks have historically been three to four times slower than even average magnetic hard-disk drives. However, several new drive technologies have increased MO drives to nearly equal hard drives in speed and data throughput. This allows you to use them for recording CD-quality audio, or small, quarter-screen digital video onto MO disks. However, the speed of MO drives has to increase drastically before you can use them to record high quality full-screen video.

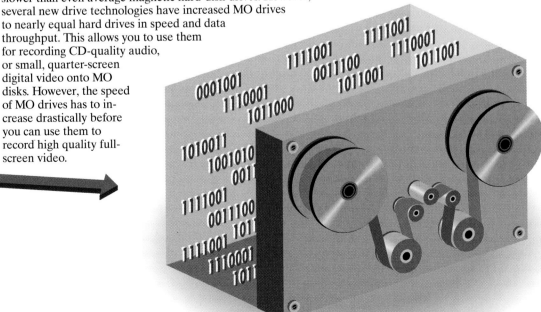

Using Tape Backup Systems in Multimedia

DAT and 8mm tape backup systems are for keeping a safe copy of all your materials during production, and then archiving the numerous media files after you've completed your project. DAT and 8mm tape are currently the most economical media for backing up the many large files that quickly fill up hard drives during multimedia production.

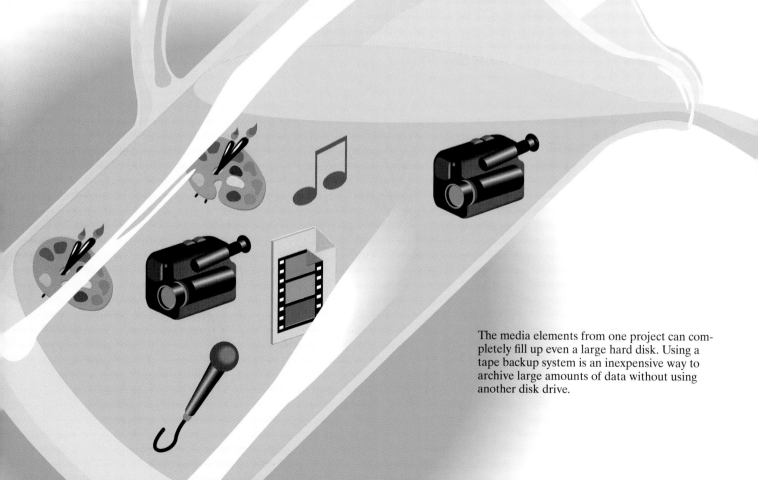

The media elements from one project can completely fill up even a large hard disk. Using a tape backup system is an inexpensive way to archive large amounts of data without using another disk drive.

PRODUCTION NOTE There are two downsides to tape backup systems: speed and fragility. Backing up a single 1GB hard drive can take a couple of hours, or even longer if several drives are being backed up over a network. DATs and 8mm tapes are also as fragile as cassette tapes, so heat, dust, and stray magnetic fields can cause data corruption. As an additional backup, many producers make backup archive copies of their data on both tape systems and either magneto-optical drives or recordable CD-ROM systems.

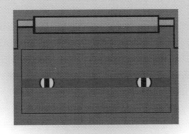

Most DATs can hold up to 1.3GB of uncompressed data, while 8mm tape can hold from 2.5GB to 5GB of uncompressed data. The label data volume on each tape brings the cost of storing data on tape down to a much lower level than that of other storage media.

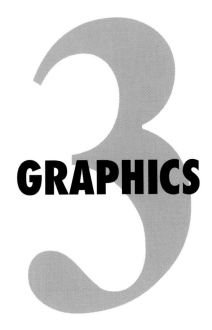

GRAPHICS

CONTENTS

ONE VERY CONSISTENT lesson in multimedia production is that people don't like reading huge amounts of text on screen. You generally can't put more than 12 to 14 lines of type on a screen without shrinking the text down to an almost unreadable level. Consequently, graphics are used more often than text to explain a concept, present background information, or improve your enjoyment when you play the title. Simply stated, while a picture is worth a thousand words, in multimedia a picture often has to substitute for a thousand words.

Video games in particular rely on good graphics. In the race to develop the best video game system, you'll often see ads by different vendors that play 8-bit, 16-bit, and even 64-bit machines against each other. The main difference between these systems is in the sophistication of their graphics, a function of their computing power.

You'll generally find several techniques and sources used to produce graphics for a multimedia title. Most artists who create graphics for multimedia titles work with a variety of tools, including a wide range of graphics software applications. You can create images in paint programs, scan in photos and hand-drawn artwork using flatbed or slide scanners, or generate three-dimensional images using 3-D modeling software. You can even combine these images using *image manipulation programs*, which can combine many different types of graphic files, to create new images or combine old ones. Probably the most popular image manipulation program of all time is Adobe Photoshop; this application is available for both the Mac and Windows machines.

Animation also plays an integral part in producing graphics for multimedia titles: video game titles tend to rely heavily on animation. The dedicated hardware built into the game machine increases animation speed as compared to most personal-computer multimedia systems. However, over the next few years this should change as hardware and software on personal computers continue to improve.

Many factors, including the user interface and the content, can affect the quality of your title. However, most producers agree on this point: The success of a multimedia title depends upon the quality of its graphics.

CHAPTER

8

Overcoming Graphics Limitations

THE MANY PLAYBACK platforms for multimedia materials make graphic production especially difficult. For the multimedia producer, the variability can be a complete nightmare. As I mentioned earlier, to ensure the success of a title, a producer needs to create versions of the title for as many platforms as possible, knowing that each platform handles graphics differently.

Some systems can show a wide range of colors, yet most are limited by the range of colors (also called *color depth*) that they can display at one time and still keep the title moving along smoothly. Other systems, such as video games, display images on video screens but not computer monitors, which places even greater limitations on image resolution and color. To make things even more complicated, each platform also uses different graphic file formats. So even if the resolution will work on another playback system, chances are the file format will not. It's not practical to create new artwork for each platform, yet each platform has its own color and resolution requirements, all of which can drastically change the original image.

To work around the file-format limitation, producers use software tools to translate graphic file formats and remap their colors. Remapping impacts an image in two ways: It changes the number of colors, and it selects the best color range, or palette. File translation in many instances is fairly easy; you simply open up a file in one format, and then save it as another format. Many graphics programs on both Mac and PC platforms have some file translation capability. A few, such as Adobe Photoshop, can translate to and from over a dozen image formats.

Remapping the colors in an image is tricky, and requires specialized software, such as DeBabelizer, a Mac-based program from Equilibrium software. Using a program like DeBabelizer allows developers to convert a 24-bit image to thousands of colors for video playback or to just 256 or fewer colors for playback on most computer systems.

When remapping colors for display on television sets, developers have to reduce not only the number of colors, but also the intensity of colors. A regular video signal, or NTSC (National Television Standards Committee) video, can't display the same vivid colors that you see on a computer screen. Often you can correct this limitation by reducing the amount, or *saturation*, of the colors in the image. However, this process results in a less vibrant graphic and represents one of the many trade-offs that multimedia developers have to face when creating a title.

How Palettes and Color Depth Changes Affect Images

Here is an example of the palette conversions that a photographic quality image has to go through before a producer can incorporate it in a multimedia title. As you move from left to right, you can see how each system limits the number of colors and the resolution that can be shown on screen.

Original 24-bit image

Mac image
(256 colors)

1 Here's an original full-color or 24-bit image. The color square on the right corner is the image's range of colors or *color palette*. Because the image is 24-bit, its color palette contains over 16.7 million colors. While 24-bit provides better images, in most cases the processing power of a playback machine CPU is not powerful enough to smoothly display the image.

2 Here the image was converted to an 8-bit or 256-color PICT file for display on an Apple Macintosh computer. Many Macs can display 24-bit images, and almost all of the Macs on the market can display 8-bit color. This PICT file was further optimized by creating an 8-bit palette that contains many of the major colors used in the image; consequently the image retains a great deal of detail.

PRODUCTION NOTE CD-ROM image collections are a prime source of graphic images for multimedia production. They can contain hundreds of beautiful still images and digitized photographs. These image collections not only offer a producer a wide variety of images to work with, but many CD-ROM collections also are royalty free.

Image courtesy of Colorbytes, Inc.

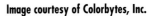

Windows image (256 colors)

Gameboy image (4 colors)

3 This shows the same image converted to an 8-bit Windows BMP file for display on a Windows computer. While both the Mac and the Windows machines use 256 colors in their palettes, they don't use the same colors; so what appears one color of red on a Mac may show up as another when the file is displayed on a PC. Again, the image has to be optimized to look good.

4 A drastic reduction in resolution and colors occurs when both the colors and resolution of the original image are reduced so the image can be displayed on a Nintendo Game Boy machine. While this is far too complex an image for most titles for this playback machine, it should give you an idea of how the image has to change to fit the playback capabilities of the media.

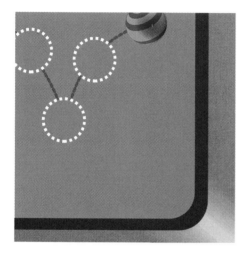

How Computer Animation Works

THE MOVEMENT IN an animation is really just an illusion. Like a movie, an animation is just a series of still images that are displayed in sequence. There are two kinds of animation in multimedia titles: two-dimensional (2-D) or cel-based animation and three-dimensional (3-D) animation. *Two-dimensional animation* or *cel animation* is the most common kind of animation, where flat images are hand-drawn one frame at a time.

While this is very time-consuming, cel animation can produce spectacular results; just look at any animated Disney film, and you'll see cel animation at its finest. Because cel animation still requires someone to draw practically every frame, many large animation houses still prefer to do it the old-fashioned way using pencils.

Computer animation has improved the inking and coloring process in cel animation; the pencil-sketched frames are colorized during this phase. In the past you had to hand-mix paint to get the right colors, and then paint in each frame on a transparent sheet or *cel*. In film, it takes 24 frames just to make one second of animation, so you can imagine how much work it took to create all the backgrounds and characters for your favorite feature-length Disney film. Digital cel painting came in about five years ago and is used extensively in animated film and television shows. Consequently, as digital cel painting becomes the standard, traditional hand-painted animation cels are becoming collector's items.

In *three-dimensional* or *3-D* animation, a mathematical model of a three-dimensional object is created to realistically portray objects with depth. (See Chapter 10 for details on 3-D animation.)

As with other types of computer graphics, hardware in your playback machine can profoundly affect how the animation in a multimedia title looks and responds.

How 2-D Animation Works

1 First the image is created, either in an external paint program or within the animation application, where you can easily adjust the object's shape and color using graphics software. The finished image is then placed on screen.

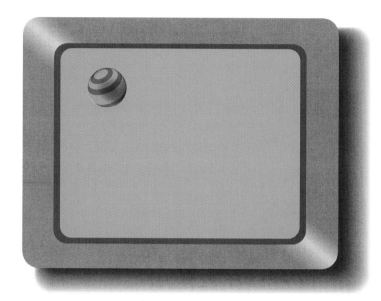

2 To create the illusion that the ball is falling, with traditional cel animation you would have to draw a ball at each different position on the screen, which is time-consuming. *In-betweening* is a feature found in 2-D animation software that eliminates this drudgery by automatically drawing the frames for you. Here the ball has been added to the same scene, but in a different location three frames later. The in-between software looks at where the object was in the first frame and then adds the extra object in between frames 1 and 3.

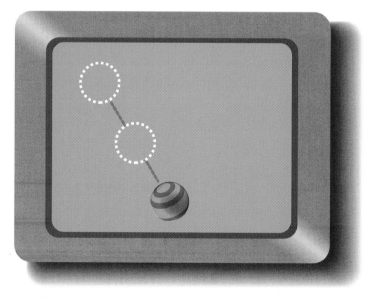

3 Using in-betweening, you can quickly animate a bouncing ball by just setting the main movement points for your animation, which constitute what is known as a *key frame*.

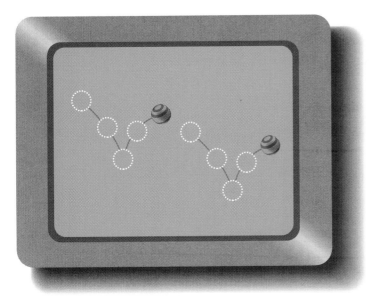

4 Animations can also contain other smaller animated characters within the program. These mini-animations are called *sprites*, and generally don't contain many frames. Here you could move a bouncing-ball sprite to anyplace on the screen; yet instead of changing the location of every frame in the ball-bouncing sequence, you just move the sprite as one unit. Wherever you move the sprite, the bouncing-ball frames will move with you. This is how many producers add animation to their video game titles, where an animated character needs to walk or move to different locations on screen.

3-D Animation

OVER THE PAST decade, 3-D animation has truly come of age. While it was once just a tool for scientific research, 3-D animation is now a common element in film, video, and multimedia productions.

Typically, in most multimedia titles, real-time 3-D animation is very limited due to the processor speed of the playback machine's CPU. The few video games that use real-time 3-D animation extensively tend to keep the graphics very simple, so that the animation can play back smoothly.

Once you've created a 3-D model, you can examine that model from any angle or distance. Many multimedia titles take advantage of this feature by creating elaborate models of entire cities or worlds for you to explore. By creating multiple views of the same model, such as a hallway, multimedia producers can create a virtual tour of their model; each time you click in a different direction, a different view of the hallway appears. It can take months to create a model that complex. However, the end result is well worth it, as seen in several multimedia titles that allow you to explore strange cities or even whole worlds for hours. For more on virtual reality, see Chapter 21.

How 3-D Animation Works

There are three stages in creating 3-D animation: modeling, animation, and rendering. Of the three, modeling and rendering take the longest to finish, as animating a 3-D object is much easier than animating a 2-D image frame by frame.

Modeling is where the 3-D object is created. There are two main directions in which you can move two-dimensional images—up (called the y-axis) and sideways (called the x-axis). In a three-dimensional model, a third axis is added: depth, or the z-axis.

OBJECT VIEW

TOP VIEW

CROSS SECTION

SIDE VIEW

Here a simple outline of a spaceship is drawn by setting coordinate points, or *vectors*. When the outline is completed, the 3-D program carves out the image like a lathe, using the outline's form to define the object's shape.

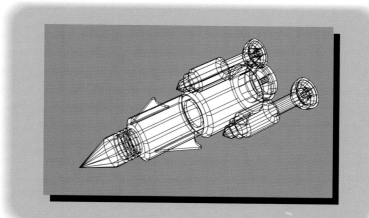

Once you've defined the z-axis, the 3-D model appears to have depth and volume. A complex model can have thousands of coordinate points, particularly if it is simulating a real object, such as a person. Sometimes this is too difficult to create by hand. For example, the model for the evil terminator in *Terminator 2: Judgment Day* was so extensive that the production staff at Industrial Light and Magic had to scan actor Robert Patrick using an ultrahigh-end laser digitizer, which created incredibly complex models of his face, head, and body.

Once the model is complete, you can also add shading and light sources to the image. Here a color and a single light have been added to the model to give it more depth. Once you change the position, scale, or angle where the light source hits, your model will also change according to where the object is in relation to the 3-D environment, which adds more realism to the model.

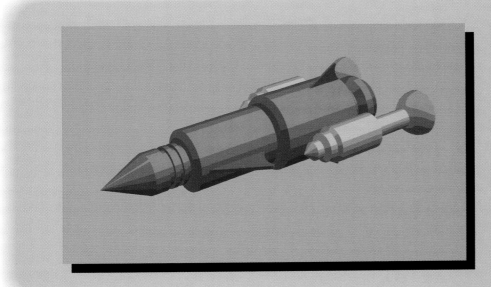

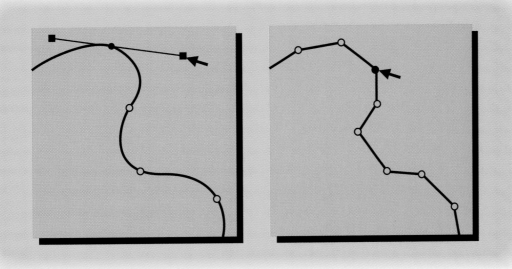

Another type of modeling that is often used to create complex shapes is *spline-based modeling*. Unlike vector-based modeling, a spline model can easily bend into complex, natural looking shapes. For example, the realistic computer-generated Tyrannosaurus Rex in the film *Jurassic Park* was created using spline-based modeling.

How 3-D Animation Works (Continued)

During animation, the 3-D model is moved along a motion path that is defined using key frames, which the 3-D animation program uses to automatically create the in-between frames in the sequence. However, unlike the key frames used in 2-D animation, in 3-D animation the position, tilt, and scale are also smoothly interpolated from key frame to key frame. This means that to create a complex animation of a spaceship curving down right and then zooming past the screen, all you would need is to adjust a few key frames, and then have the program create the in-between frames of the sequence.

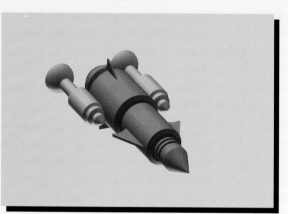

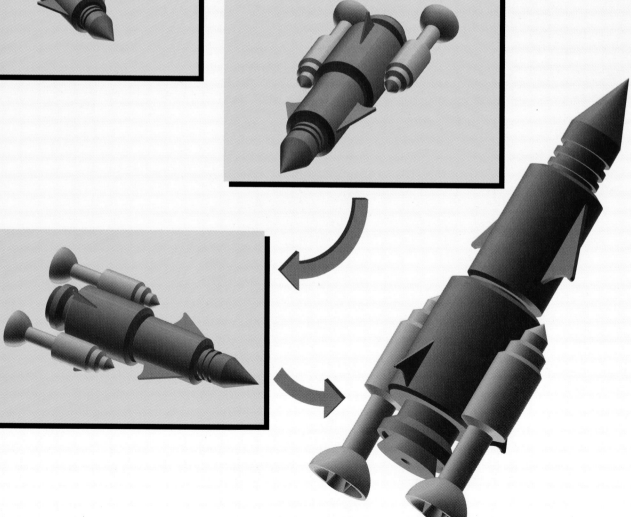

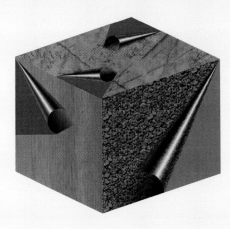

Rendering is the final stage in creating a 3-D animation, and often the stage that takes the longest to complete. Blending texture maps into the model to add realism causes one of the main slowdowns during rendering. A *texture map* is really just wallpaper for 3-D models, in which a graphic image is wrapped over the surface of a model. Unlike real wallpaper, the texture map smoothly blends over every nook and cranny in the image to give the illusion that it is a part of the model.

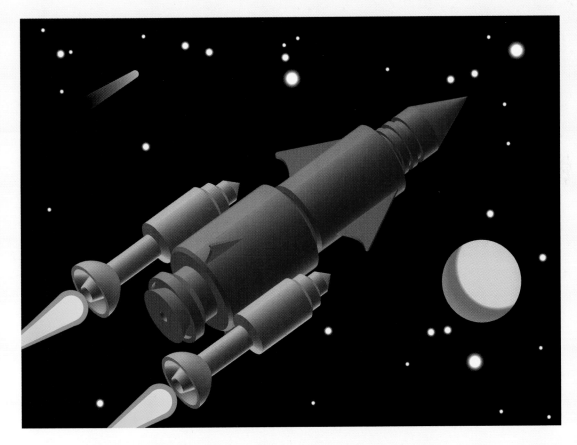

When a 3-D animation program renders an image, it blends all the light sources, background images, texture maps, and surface attributes in each frame of a 3-D animation sequence. All this graphical information is saved as individual frames for later output either to videotape or for compiling into a digital movie.

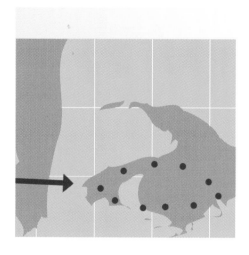

How Morphing Works

MORPHING AND WARPING are two special effects that are finding their way into more multimedia titles. *Morphing* is a special effect that takes two images and seamlessly changes one image into another; the second image actually seems to grow out of the first one. This effect can be startling when used with vastly different images.

You're probably very familiar with morphing effects because they are seen in many different motion pictures, television shows, and videos. The changing faces at the end of Michael Jackson's "Black and White" music video, the evil terminator in *Terminator 2: Judgment Day*, and the shape-shifting security chief on "Star Trek: Deep Space Nine" are all examples of morphing.

Showing change over time is probably the best use of morphing. Instead of just displaying a "before" and "after" photo of something, morphing software lets you see the change occur gradually. When applied to product research, this is a great way to analyze all the changes that a company has integrated over a period of years. For example, by morphing the profiles on different years of the same model of car, you can show all the stylistic changes in the car's design.

Morphing can also show the pace of change more clearly than photos. Using the same example, you might see the shape of the doors change quite radically, but find that the trim design around the wheels has changed very little over the years. In medicine, researchers can use this same approach on medical images to analyze the spread of disease in the body, while documenting the areas that remain unaffected.

Warping is a variation of morphing, where only one image changes over time. For example, using warping you could take a row of glasses and cause them to wilt like old flowers, or make a person's head puff out like a balloon. Of course, you can make much more subtle warping changes. For example, with a little creative warping, you can take a frown and transform it into a smile.

As with all special effects, it's easy to overuse morphing and warping, and numb the audience to the effect. However, in the right context, morphing and warping are powerful ways to show change.

How Morphing Works

Essentially, morphing uses a map of both images to move the pixels in both pictures while simultaneously blending the images.

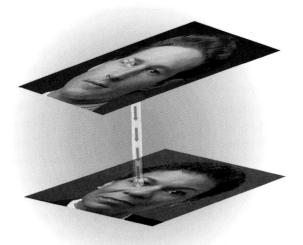

1 First a series of coordinates or key points is set up in both the start and end images, so that the location of an object such as an eye in the start image is matched to the location of the eye on the end image. You keep applying key points until at least all the main features in your image such as the eyes, ears, mouth, and shape of head are mapped out. The more points or coordinates that you add, the smoother the blend between the two images.

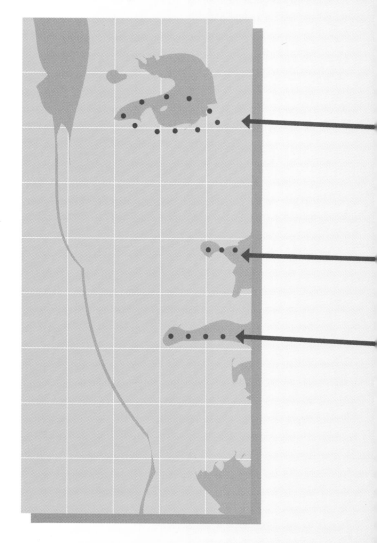

2 Once the coordinates are set, the morphing software algorithm pushes the pixels mapped out in the start image to their final destination in the end image while blending or *interpolating* the image colors and shapes.

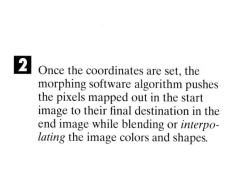

Image courtesy of ASDG, Inc. Morphing effects created by Dave Lauer.

3 Here the image of one person is transformed into another. Note the way that the jacket seems to be pulled onto the man during the morph just a little faster than the face changes. Some of the high-end software packages can precisely control the rate and amount that some areas are affected by the morphing algorithms.

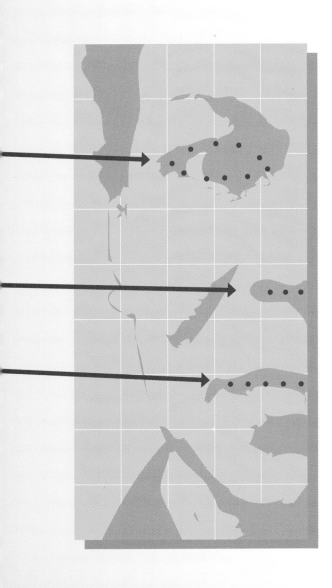

How Warping Works

Warping uses the key points of one image to create different effects, instead of blending two images together. You can push the pixels of the original image into different shapes just by readjusting the key points of the original image.

1 As with morphing, warping takes and maps a set of coordinates from one image to another. The difference is that warping does not blend the original image into a second image, but simply moves the pixels in the original image to new locations.

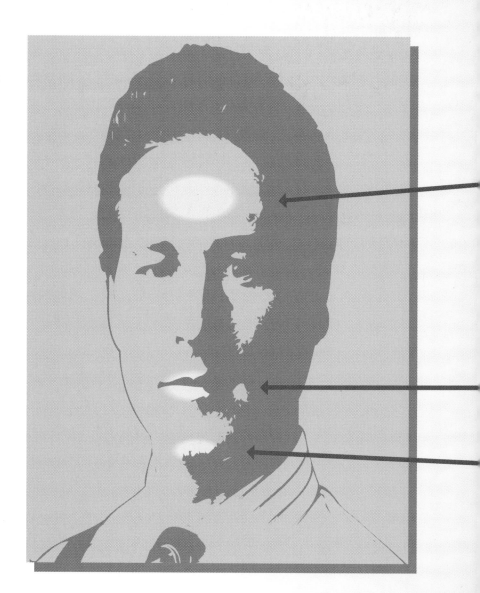

Image courtesy of ASDG, Inc. Warping effect created by Erik Holsinger.

2 In the final warp, our corporate executive is magically transformed into a corporate elf by warping effects. During the warp, his face became narrower and his hair was pushed up and squared off; his mouth and shoulders were reduced; his lips were pushed into a smile; his ears sprouted points; and his chin and forehead were stretched.

UNDERSTANDING DIGITAL VIDEO

4

CONTENTS

DIGITAL VIDEO TECHNOLOGY has been around for several years, but is just now on the verge of breaking into the mainstream as the standard way that we play back and record video in multimedia applications. This is an event that many people in the television and video production industries have anticipated for decades. Believe it or not—despite major advances in communications, computer, and video technology—television is still using a video standard that is over 40 years old!

In 1941, the National Television Standards Committee (NTSC) approved the first standard for black-and-white television; 12 years later, in 1953, they added color to the black-and-white signal. This standard (called NTSC video) made color video compatible with the millions of black-and-white television sets already on the market. However, because the color was piggybacked onto the black-and-white signal, they had to limit the amount of color information that could be displayed. Consequently, the same vibrant colors that you see on a computer monitor are too vibrant for regular NTSC video.

Digital video offers a number of improvements over a standard NTSC video signal, including a much better range of colors. The typical NTSC video signal can show only about 32,000 colors, while many computer monitors can display photo-realistic images that contain over 16 million colors.

Unlike regular video, digital video image quality won't degrade from copy to copy. When you make a copy of a videotape, you'll notice that the picture isn't as good as the original; make a copy of the copy and the image gets even worse because the image recorded onto the videotape loses information about what makes up the signal every time it is copied. Even many videotape formats that producers use in professional video production begin to lose quality after just five or six copies (also called *generations*).

Because digital video is made up of a digital code and not an electrical analog signal, a digital video copy contains the exact information as the original. As long as the signal stays in its digital format, you can go an endless number of generations before you see any discernible drop in image quality.

Like film, television quickly shows many still images (called *frames*) one after another to produce the illusion of movement. To make up for the deficiencies in early television monitor tubes, the *interlaced* video signal splits each frame into two segments, called *fields*, to keep the image from flickering.

Unfortunately, we're still stuck with interlaced video, even though monitor display technology has long since moved beyond this system. Displaying very thin lines, which is a breeze on a computer monitor, is a pain on video monitors. A superthin single-pixel line can get scanned in one field, but is left out when the television picture tube scans the next field; this causes the line to flicker madly, even though it's not moving. Next time you watch television, look for a still image where the edges seem to jitter; if they do, you're seeing an example of interlaced video artifacts. Just about every computer monitor on the market uses a noninterlaced signal free from all or most of the quirks associated with an interlaced signal. Digital video systems could help free video from the interlaced standard.

Finally, and most importantly, you can compress digital video into many different sizes depending upon how you use it. For example, when you edit together video sequences, you'll use very little video compression to keep the image quality as clean as possible. Later, after you've edited together all the digital video sequences, you can again compress the whole digital video sequence so it will play back smoothly from CD-ROM or even from video game cartridges.

The distribution potential for digital video is perhaps the greatest benefit in the switch-over from digital to analog systems. Because a digital video file is just another type of binary computer data, you can now find digital video in all kinds of multimedia programs, from education titles to interactive video games.

Cable television companies are especially interested in digital video, because they can use it to distribute huge amounts of programming over your regular cable line. The digital video signal takes up less bandwidth than a regular video signal; a cable TV company could fit up to three digital video signals into just one cable television channel. One service that could arise is *video-on-demand*: You could call your local cable station to order a digital video sent at a time of your choice. With enough digital video storage, you could have a pay-per-view service with hundreds of selections available at one time.

Ultimately, if you do still go to the store to rent a video, you might find that the store has replaced the videotapes with digital Video CD-ROMs. Video CD-ROMs have many potential advantages over VHS tape. It costs only about $1.50 to duplicate a CD-ROM compared to the $4 to $6 that it takes to make a copy of a videotape. Also, like an audio CD, a Video CD-ROM can last for many years without either the video or the audio degrading. Most videotapes start losing quality after about 35 viewings; a Video CD-ROM would keep going long after most videotapes break down. Because of the high amount of compression needed to play back a digital video from CD-ROMs, the quality of a Video CD-ROM's digital video is not as good as what you can find on laser discs. However, eventually this will change: Chances are the VCR of the future will use CD-ROMs—and not videotape—to play back your favorite shows.

Understanding Digital Video in Multimedia

WHILE MANY TYPES of technology played a part in the development of interactive technology, the addition of digital video to personal computers was one of the big milestones in multimedia. Now producers can use video segments to demonstrate job tasks, play back interviews, show cause and effect over time, and otherwise add interest to their titles. Getting the video into your title, however, is not easy.

During production, how you initially convert the video will determine the quality of the final digital video sequence in a multimedia title. You'll immediately see a number of problems in a badly digitized file, such as missing frames or bad color resolution from too much initial compression. Producers have to correct these problems before digitizing the final sequence, otherwise they are stuck with a flawed digital video sequence throughout production.

Generally you'll need to compress all digital video files several times at different quality levels, depending upon where you are in the production process. Initially, the compression is kept very low to maximize image quality. To create fast previews during testing, you create very small-sized movies with medium compression settings. Once you are satisfied with your movie file, you then save it with a very high compression level. The higher the compression, the less data the storage device has to pass to the computer, which means faster and smoother video playback.

Most of the time, these movies use whatever digital movie software is available. On the Mac, you would use QuickTime, while on the PC you might use Video for Windows. There are several other compression systems that are specific to different hardware digitizing cards, such as JPEG and MPEG (see Chapters 13 and 14). Also, producers must heavily compress digital video files for playback from a CD-ROM. On the Mac, they would use the Compact Video compression scheme, while for the PC they would use the Indeo. Both of these software algorithms limit the data rate of the digital video file.

For playback, a digital video movie is started from a separate utility (such as the Movie Player software on the Mac or the Media Player utility for Windows-based machines), from an authoring application, or from some other type of stand-alone application.

How Video Is Digitized

Video and audio come in from a video source, either a camera or VCR, to the audio and video digitizer cards inside a computer. On some systems both the audio and video digitizing functions are on one card.

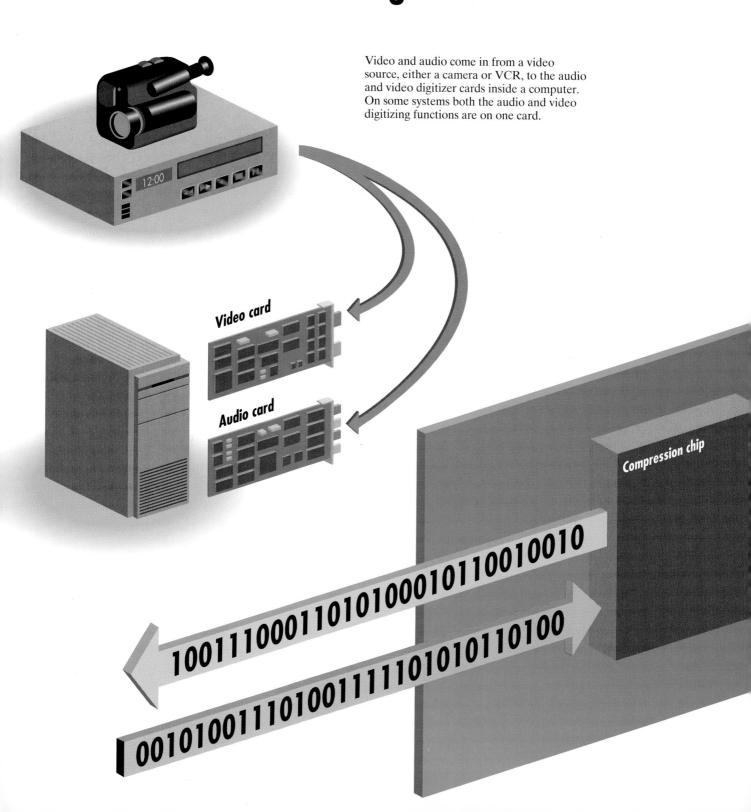

Video card

Audio card

Compression chip

10011100011010100010110010010

0010100111010011111101010110100

Using a process called *sampling*, the analog-to-digital (A/D) converters on the cards process the analog video and audio signals into digital data streams. Sampling is the process that changes the video and audio signals into a binary data structure of 1's and 0's that exists in all computer media.

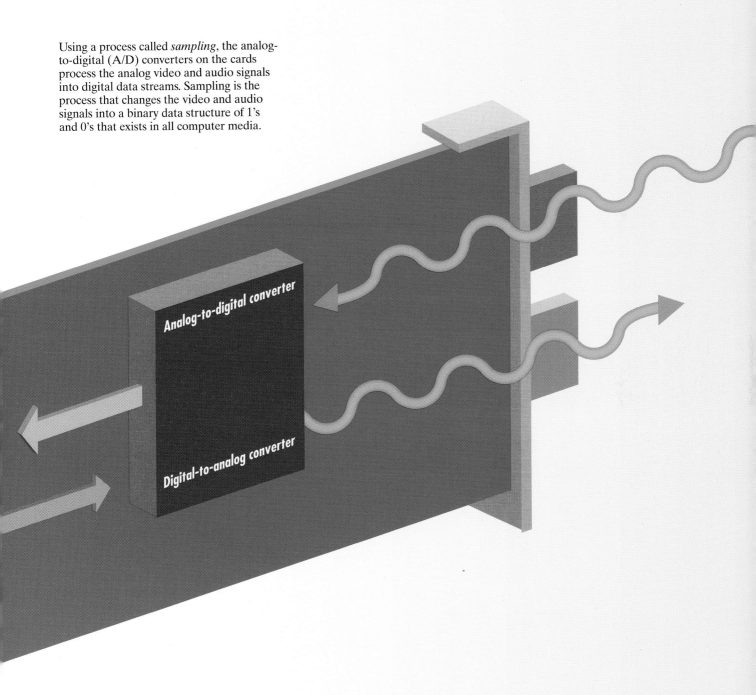

Analog-to-digital converter

Digital-to-analog converter

How Video Is Digitized (continued)

Hardware video compressor on digitizer card

The size of the digital data stream is then drastically reduced using some type of image data compression, such as JPEG or MPEG. This can reduce the size of the file by as much as 200 percent. The audio remains uncompressed, which enables you to have high quality audio with heavily compressed digital video.

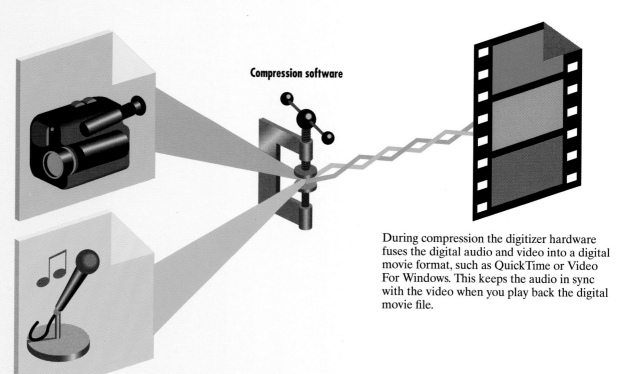

Compression software

During compression the digitizer hardware fuses the digital audio and video into a digital movie format, such as QuickTime or Video For Windows. This keeps the audio in sync with the video when you play back the digital movie file.

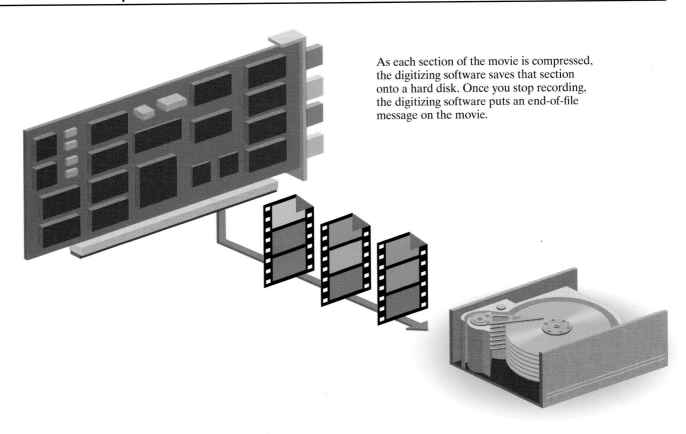

As each section of the movie is compressed, the digitizing software saves that section onto a hard disk. Once you stop recording, the digitizing software puts an end-of-file message on the movie.

Once the digital movie is completed, you can play back the digitized movie on your computer screen. If the movie uses a custom compression scheme that is designed specifically for the digitizer card, the file is sent back through the digitizer hardware to speed up the playback of the file.

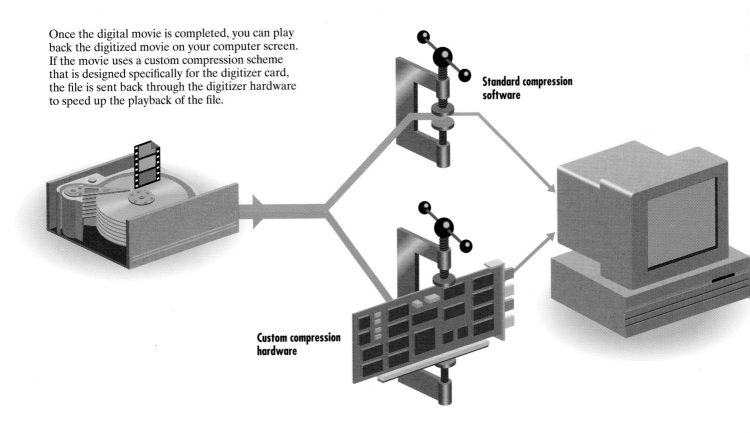

Standard compression software

Custom compression hardware

CHAPTER

Understanding JPEG Compression

THE JPEG (JOINT PHOTOGRAPHIC EXPERTS GROUP) compression algorithm removes redundant picture information from photographs and other types of still images. When C-Cube Microsystems developed one of the first hardware JPEG compression chips for still images, they found (much to their surprise) that their JPEG chip compressed and decompressed still images in $\frac{1}{30}$th of a second. Consequently, when combined with digitizer hardware, JPEG hardware compression systems can compress images fast enough to play and record video at 30 frames per second. JPEG is the key compression technology behind most of the hardware that can play back full-screen digital movies, especially on the Macintosh platform.

To give you a better idea of how JPEG works, here's an example of how JPEG would look if you could apply it to some text:

Ths is a gd exampl of dta comprssn: Jst enoug dta to gt th pont acrss.

You can comprehend the above sentence because your mind fills in the missing letters, or pieces. So while we've reduced the length of the sentence by removing a few letters, nothing is lost in the *content* of the sentence. JPEG works exactly the same way; it saves only the amount of information necessary to restore the original image.

There are two things developers have to keep in mind when working with JPEG compression. First, JPEG can make an image up to 100 times smaller than the original file (called a 100:1 ratio), but the image quality at that level is not good. At 20:1 compression, you will see little change in an image. However, when you get past a 20:1 JPEG compression, you will generally see the image begin to degrade, which shows up as artifacts within the original image.

Another thing to remember is that JPEG schemes are either lossy or lossless schemes. *Lossy* JPEG loses some image information each time it compresses an image, while *lossless* JPEG compression will record all the image data every time. Most JPEG systems are lossy, because lossy JPEG algorithms provide better compression ratios than lossless JPEG.

How JPEG Works

JPEG breaks the pixels of the image down into blocks of common colors. So instead of remembering each pixel in this section of background, JPEG simply takes a single reference on the color and position of the section.

In this picture, you'd think that there are all kinds of color detail in the image. In fact there is a lot of repeated information—such as the color of the background and the color of the ground. JPEG removes this redundant information, taking out just enough information to be able to put back together the image when decompressed.

As you apply more compression, the JPEG algorithm stores less information per scene. This 24-bit color image normally takes up 11.2MB, which would fill about eight high-density floppy disks.

Original image (11.2MB)

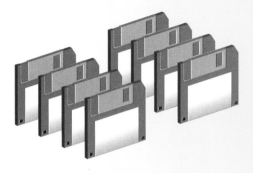

Using an 8:1 ratio of JPEG compression, you can reduce the file size of the image so that it can fit on one floppy disk. At this ratio, you lose very little image quality.

8:1 compression (1.4MB)

By the time you've hit 100:1 compression levels, the image will be barely recognizable. However, this is not as big an issue with digital video. When you look at the digital video sequence, your eyes can't grasp the lack of distinct details of each individual frame. To make up for this, your eyes fill in the missing details, so you only see a slight blurry quality to the image, instead of the blocky pixelized look that you see here.

100:1 compression (11K)

PRODUCTION NOTE There are two other ways that producers reduce the file size of digital video using JPEG compression. Instead of recording all 30 frames per second (the standard rate in video), some producers will record only every other frame (15 frames per second) or even every third frame (10 frames per second). The other way to drastically reduce the file size of a digital move is to reduce its size on screen. This is why most video games only show digital movies at about a quarter of the screen size.

Image courtesy of ColorBytes, Inc. Photograph by Bob Barber.

C H A P T E R
14

Inside MPEG Video Compression

WHILE YOU CAN get very high compression ratios with JPEG, in many cases they're not high enough. As mentioned in the previous chapter, you can get 100:1 compression with JPEG, but it looks awful. However, full-motion digital video really needs as much compression as possible if it is going to fit on most standard storage devices—especially CD-ROM discs. That's where MPEG comes in. Like JPEG, MPEG (Moving Pictures Expert Group) is a compression algorithm that reduces redundant information in images. However, MPEG provides compression levels up to 200:1 with extremely high quality images and sound.

MPEG compression is very asymmetrical; in some cases it can take as much as one hour to compress one minute of video. JPEG compression is somewhat symmetrical in its compression and decompression. In other words, decompressing and compressing an image should take about the same amount of time. The advantage of using MPEG compression over JPEG is that digital movies will run faster and take up less space.

Indeo is another type of compression found primarily on PCs and Windows hardware and is very similar to MPEG. Originally called DVI (Digital Video Interactive), Indeo is a digital video standard developed by Intel for the IBM PC market many years ago. DVI was never really adopted by the PC community because of two fatal flaws—it required specialized hardware just to play back images, and movies had to be sent to Intel to be compressed by their mainframe computers. Indeo uses a brand-new chip set from Intel Corporation that has newer and better compression algorithms, including MPEG.

One thing that's important to remember about both MPEG and Indeo is they are distribution formats, not designed for editing digital video. This is because it is difficult to randomly access individual frames within an MPEG-based movie. MPEG and Indeo compression are formats that were made to squeeze moving video into the smallest possible files. With smaller files, producers can play back video from a wide range of storage devices, especially CD-ROM. However, you cannot edit these files as you can edit JPEG files because each frame is greatly dependent upon other frames for its information. If you wanted to see an individual frame, you'd have to construct the frame from several adjoining frames.

MPEG is dependent upon hardware to compress and decompress movies. Many vendors have already announced plans to bring out MPEG hardware for both computer and home video game technology.

How MPEG Compares to JPEG

JPEG

Key frame

JPEG compresses images by getting rid of redundant information within a frame (which is called *intraframe* compression). MPEG also uses intraframe compression, but further reduces each frame with *interframe* compression, which reduces the redundant information between frames.

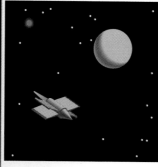  

⟵ **14 frames** ⟶

While JPEG will compress every frame, MPEG actually compresses only the key information, such as background images and so on, every 15th frame or half second. The rest of the time the MPEG algorithm only records the changes between the two frames. The movement of the rocket and the spinning planet are really the only things that are changing, so their movement will be the only thing that the MPEG algorithm will record between key frames, which are redefined frames in a sequence and reference points in an animation or digital movie.

MPEG

Key frame

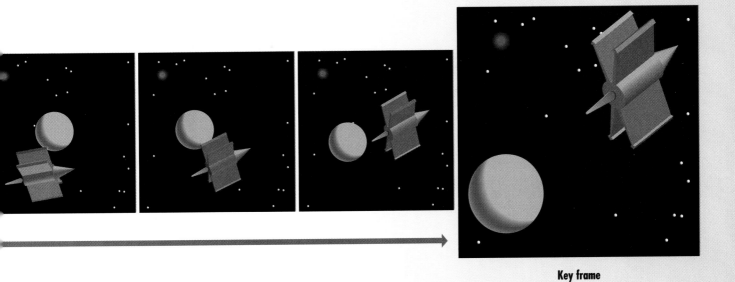

Key frame

Only movement is recorded.

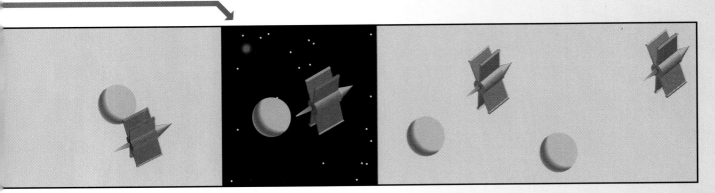

Key frame

CHAPTER 15

Nonlinear Video Editing

VIDEOTAPE REALLY only works one way: You put the tape in, and it plays from start to finish. This "linear" mode is fine for playing movies on videotape, but it's a pain in the neck when you have to edit video sequences together for a multimedia production. Every time you make major changes in the sequence order, you have to redo a program from scratch; you can't change something at the beginning of a videotape and have all of the other material adapt to this change.

Nonlinear editing systems revolutionized the video editing process in the same way word processing systems forever changed the way we write documents. Remember when you had to type everything on a typewriter? You couldn't make major changes without retyping the document or drenching it in correction fluid. With word processors, you now make changes to the electronic copy on the computer screen. No matter how extensive the changes, the text in your document flows around the added or deleted text automatically. If you are not happy with the document, just change the electronic copy and print it as many times as you like. A nonlinear editing system allows you to cut and paste digital video in any order and create as many versions as you choose. You can start at the end (or any other point in your show), and work forward or backward, adding material as needed.

Digital video footage offers another advantage over regular videotape: random access of footage. Unlike a videotape, which must be fast-forwarded or rewound to get to different sections of the tape, you can play digitized video on a hard disk instantly. (The illustration in this chapter shows how this is done.) For editors, this speed increase can cut down by more than 50 percent the time it takes to edit a program.

The image quality of nonlinear systems varies widely and depends upon how much compression is applied to the video sequence after it is digitized. The amount of footage you can work with and the quality of the signal are controlled by the amount of compression used on the video. Add compression, and you reduce both the quality of the image and the size of the video file. The most expensive systems on the market from Avid Technology, ImMIX, and others can provide excellent image quality. However, these systems compromise on the amount of video that they can store: Some systems can hold only minutes, not hours, of video. Still, not only can nonlinear video editing systems increase speed, but they can also enhance the creativity that editors bring to the final video editing post-prodcution process.

Nonlinear versus Traditional Editing

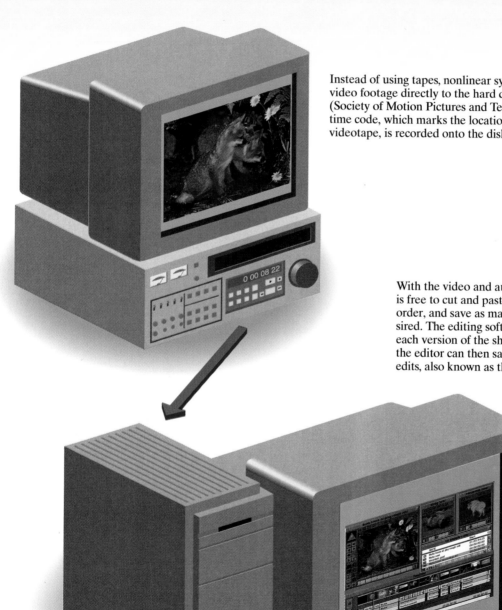

Instead of using tapes, nonlinear systems record the video footage directly to the hard disk. The *SMPTE* (Society of Motion Pictures and Television Engineers) time code, which marks the location of each frame on the videotape, is recorded onto the disk at the same time.

With the video and audio in digital form, the editor is free to cut and paste sections together in any order, and save as many versions of the show as desired. The editing software notes every edit made in each version of the show. When the edit is approved, the editor can then save to disk or print the list of edits, also known as the *EDL* (Edit Decision List).

Like a desktop publishing layout program, nonlinear systems don't place the actual digitized video files into each EDL. Instead, the software uses the EDL to mark where in the digitized file the specific audio or video can be found. An editor can then reassemble the program in a high-end video editing center (also called an on-line suite) using the EDL to conform the original tapes to the edit completed in the nonlinear edit session.

Traditional Video Editing

In traditional video editing, removing the middle segment leaves a gap between the first and last segments. Conversely, adding a new segment to the end of the first segment will erase most of the last segment.

Nonlinear Editing

If you remove a key segment at the beginning of your video, the nonlinear software will automatically fill the gap left by the segment with the video segment that comes after that gap. This way you don't have to start from scratch and move over the original material. It's the equivalent of making changes to a word-processed memo; you can just reorder or reorganize the text without retyping the page. Nonlinear editing systems allow you to edit your show together in any order you desire.

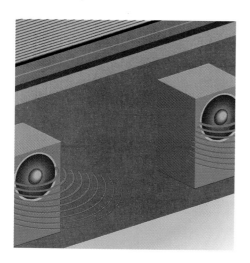

Understanding HDTV

HDTV (HIGH Definition Television) is the latest evolution of the video signal that uses a wide-screen 16:9 image ratio and doubles the vertical resolution to up to 1,150 lines. High definition television is a far greater change over our current video system than the move from black-and-white to color television. Not only does HDTV drastically improve image quality, but its increased image size and audio fidelity could also help transform the standard television into a more movie-like experience.

Unlike traditional NTSC video, HDTV is a digital video signal. The biggest difference between HDTV and NTSC is the quality and size of the image. HDTV doubles the vertical image resolution in the video signal, for incredibly bright and sharp images. An HDTV screen is also much wider than a regular television screen, with a wide 16:9 movie-screen format. Have you ever seen a movie in "letter-box" format on TV? The 16:9 ratio of HDTV will replace the black strips on the top and bottom of the screen with a larger and more clear image. Unlike the cramped 4:3 dimensions of regular video, no cropping is necessary when transferring 35mm motion pictures to HDTV. In fact, many experts in the film and television industry feel that HDTV will be the ultimate film-to-video transfer format, which could mean that a variety of transferred 35mm films could be available shortly after HDTV is finally ready to broadcast. Lastly, an HDTV signal contains four channels of CD-quality sound, for surround-sound or multiple language programs.

However, HDTV is not without its problems, and most experts agree that it will be several years before HDTV becomes a household name. One of the biggest strikes against HDTV is the high cost of the technology. Initially HDTV video equipment for consumers will cost 50 to 100 percent more than most consumer electronic devices. Still, several companies have announced plans to market HDTV consumer and professional products at a fraction of their current cost when they hit U.S. shores.

Three years ago, a plain-vanilla HDTV video monitor could cost you over $35,000 when purchased in Japan. Today several FCC studies show that when HDTV finally comes to the U.S., the cost for a large 54-inch consumer projection TV will be around $3,900, while a 34-inch HDTV receiver will set you back around $2,600. Once full-scale production gets under way, vendors will be able to reduce their costs and the final consumer prices even further.

How HDTV Works

The enhanced resolution of HDTV provides an incredibly sharp image with more vibrant colors than any normal video signal. The contrast range is better than that of regular television; even when shot in dimly lit areas, the HDTV signal is remarkably robust and clear when compared to an NTSC composite video signal of the same image.

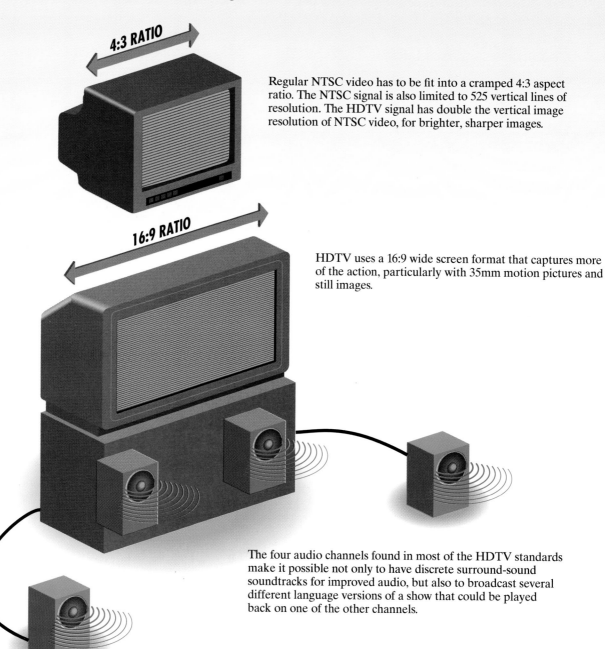

Regular NTSC video has to be fit into a cramped 4:3 aspect ratio. The NTSC signal is also limited to 525 vertical lines of resolution. The HDTV signal has double the vertical image resolution of NTSC video, for brighter, sharper images.

HDTV uses a 16:9 wide screen format that captures more of the action, particularly with 35mm motion pictures and still images.

The four audio channels found in most of the HDTV standards make it possible not only to have discrete surround-sound soundtracks for improved audio, but also to broadcast several different language versions of a show that could be played back on one of the other channels.

How HDTV Programming Will Reach Your Home

After a broadcast station has upgraded its facilities to HDTV capabilities, there are several ways that you could receive programming.

The broadcast station could send the digital HDTV signal over the air to a specific broadcast area. Unlike regular television, with HDTV you could get a full-strength signal no matter where you were in the broadcast area.

At the same time, the broadcast station could send the signal to your cable operator so they could relay the signal as a cable TV signal. This same signal could also be sent via an advanced phone line and linked directly into your computer.

A third version of the signal also could go out that would convert the HDTV signal to regular NTSC. This would allow you to enjoy HDTV programming even if you didn't have an HDTV television set.

UNDERSTANDING DIGITAL AUDIO

CONTENTS

FROM THE MOMENT the talkies were invented, audio—especially music and sound effects—has been a big part of movies and television. These days the major enhancements to motion picture theater technology are focused primarily on the audio system.

Audio is also vital in multimedia; without the right sound effects or music, a program doesn't have nearly as much appeal. This is because sound effects and music greatly enhance the interactivity of the multimedia title. For example, clicking on a button in a program will bring up a new screen. However, if you hear a "click" or "whir" sound the moment you click that same button, suddenly the experience has changed. Hearing a sound after clicking a button makes it clear that you caused an action. This is one way in which producers use audio to confirm actions and enhance interactivity within a title.

Of all the technologies involved in creating a multimedia title, digital audio is perhaps the easiest to implement. This is partly because digital audio technology has been in the mainstream for many years now in the form of compact discs. The same technology that you used to play your CDs is now available for computer and consumer multimedia systems at a fraction of what they cost years ago. This has significantly improved the quality of multimedia titles, which now can add a unique sonic atmosphere of electrifying sound effects and music to hold your interest.

Of course, not all digital audio systems can play back the same quality of audio that you hear on your home CD system. In fact, the digital audio systems built into most personal computer and video game systems have all the audio fidelity of a telephone. Sampling is responsible for the variation in audio fidelity. *Sampling* is the process of converting a sound from analog to digital audio, and is covered in the first chapter in this section.

MIDI (Musical Instrument Digital Interface) is another important audio technology used in multimedia production. MIDI is not a digital audio signal, but is actually a communications standard that enables computers and electronic music instruments to talk to each other. Producers often use MIDI-based studios to create music that is later digitized for use in a title. However, new low-cost MIDI devices are now available that you can hook up to personal computers to further enhance some multimedia titles.

Eventually, both digital audio and MIDI technologies will be a part of computer and consumer multimedia playback systems. However, for now the most sophisticated digital audio and MIDI equipment is in the domain of the multimedia producer.

How Audio Is Digitized

PRODUCERS HAVE TO convert audio to a digital form in order to use it in multimedia titles as they do with video. Sampling is used to convert analog audio to digital audio. A decade ago, the technology required for performing this conversion was very expensive. Today sampling hardware and software is a very cost effective add-on for computer and consumer multimedia systems. Once the audio has been sampled, or digitized, you can play it back from your computer. The digital audio system will then have to reconvert the digital audio sample back into an analog audio signal so you can hear it on speakers.

This two-way transformation process is called analog-to-digital (A/D) conversion when you record digital audio, and digital-to-analog (D/A) conversion when you play it back. You hear high-end sampling and D/A conversion every time you listen to music recorded on a compact disc. The music's original analog audio signal is sampled at 44.1 kHz when the master audio recording is transferred to CD. Each time you play your CD, the CD player converts the digital audio file back into an analog signal so that you can hear the CD over your speakers.

While recording companies sample at 44.1, the range of human hearing stops at about 20 kHz. As a rule of thumb, the highest frequency of sound that you can play back from a sample is less than half the rate at which you sampled the sound. Recording companies sample at 44.1 to ensure that the audio on your CDs is "CD-quality." (See the first illustration in this chapter.)

Generally, multimedia producers have to make a lot of compromises when using digital audio. While CD-quality digital audio sounds great, it takes up a lot of space—about 10MB or seven high-density floppy disks for just one minute of stereo audio. To get around this, producers will often record sound effects and even dialogue at a much lower sample rates and resolutions. While the sound quality is diminished, this can greatly increase the number of sounds used in a multimedia title.

How Audio Is Digitized

The digitization process of audio is rather simple. It's really just a matter of converting an electrical signal to a computer data file. Here a microphone converts the sound waves from a person's voice into an electrical signal which is called an analog audio signal. The analog signal is then routed into the audio inputs on a digital audio card. The audio could just as easily come from a tape player or radio—virtually any source that can output an analog audio signal.

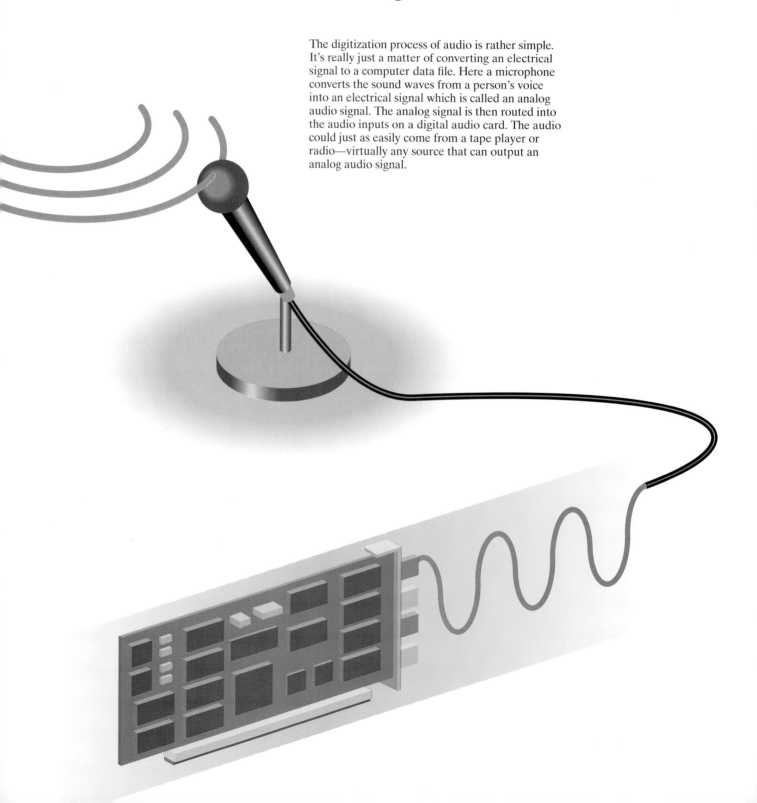

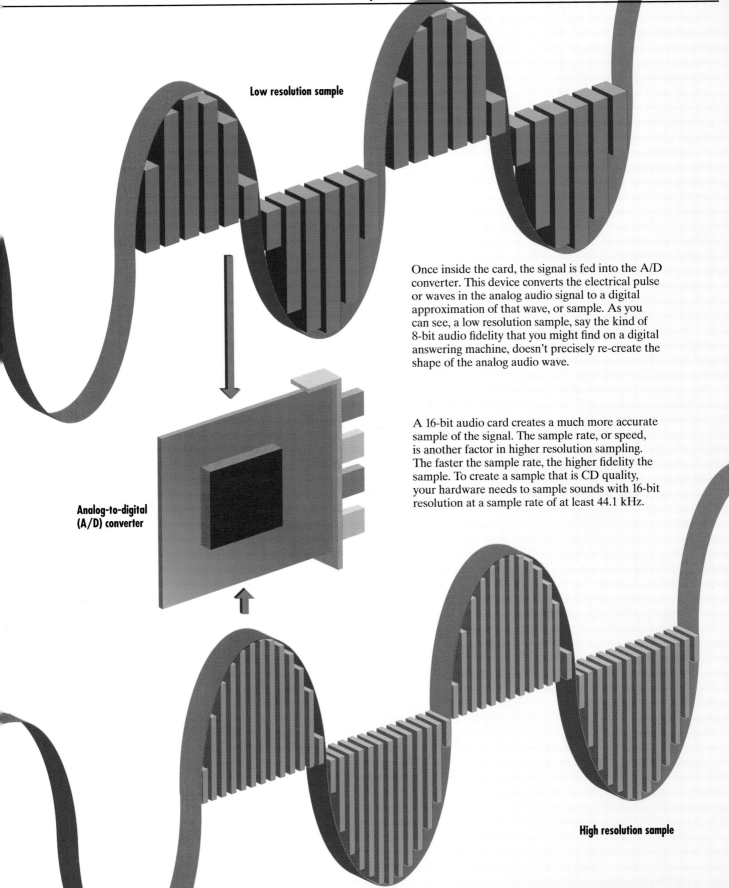

Low resolution sample

Analog-to-digital (A/D) converter

High resolution sample

Once inside the card, the signal is fed into the A/D converter. This device converts the electrical pulse or waves in the analog audio signal to a digital approximation of that wave, or sample. As you can see, a low resolution sample, say the kind of 8-bit audio fidelity that you might find on a digital answering machine, doesn't precisely re-create the shape of the analog audio wave.

A 16-bit audio card creates a much more accurate sample of the signal. The sample rate, or speed, is another factor in higher resolution sampling. The faster the sample rate, the higher fidelity the sample. To create a sample that is CD quality, your hardware needs to sample sounds with 16-bit resolution at a sample rate of at least 44.1 kHz.

How Audio Is Digitized (Continued)

Playing back a digital audio file is the reverse of the recording process. Once you send the digital audio file to the card for playback, the file is routed back through a converter, only this time the digitized version of the file is changed into an analog signal.

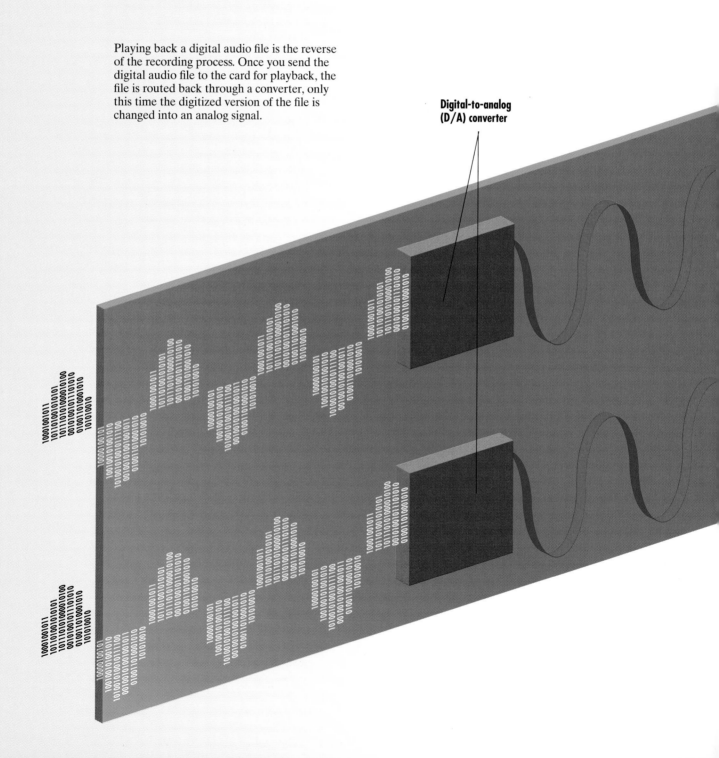

Digital-to-analog (D/A) converter

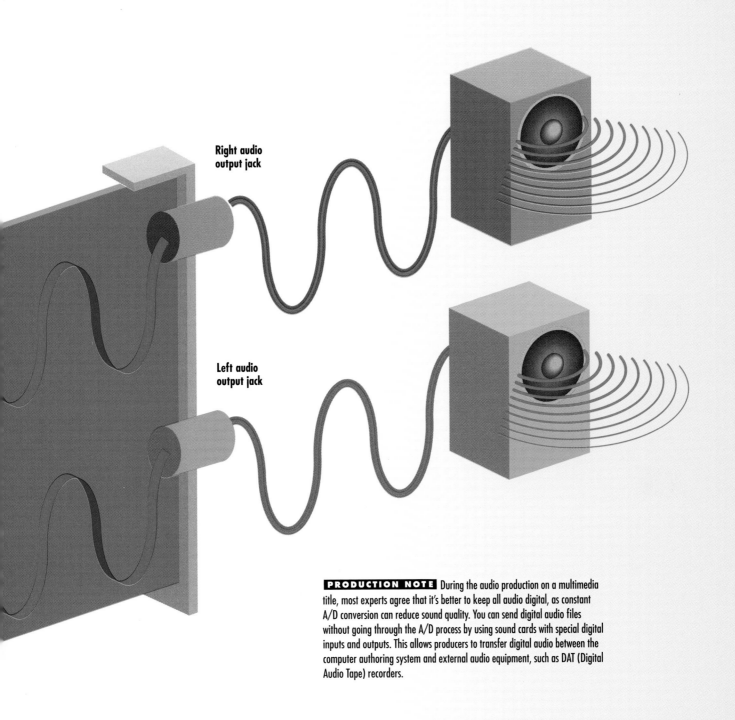

Right audio output jack

Left audio output jack

PRODUCTION NOTE During the audio production on a multimedia title, most experts agree that it's better to keep all audio digital, as constant A/D conversion can reduce sound quality. You can send digital audio files without going through the A/D process by using sound cards with special digital inputs and outputs. This allows producers to transfer digital audio between the computer authoring system and external audio equipment, such as DAT (Digital Audio Tape) recorders.

How Multimedia Applications Play Back Digital Sound

AUDIO PLAYBACK HARDWARE in multimedia systems has long taken a back seat to video hardware. While many computer systems can display photo-realistic graphics on a computer monitor, few have decent sound capabilities built-in. This is especially true of the early IBM PCs and compatibles, which could barely manage a "beep" tone through a small internal speaker. However, the multimedia systems on the market today have much-improved audio capabilities. Most of these products are from third-party vendors that manufacture miniature powered speakers and digital audio boards.

The internal sound playback capabilities of nearly all computer systems are still managed through a single internal speaker, yet the output capabilities of each system are rather diverse. For example, many Mac systems include digital audio in and out stereo capabilities, as well as a built-in internal speaker. IBM PCs and compatibles are generally limited to just a small internal speaker, although many third-party vendors offer low-cost audio output boards and external speaker systems. Overall, you can improve the quality of any sound coming from a personal computer if you bypass the internal speaker on the computer and output the sound directly to a set of powered speakers or a home stereo system.

Some authoring and playback systems include a small audio mixer, particularly if your multimedia title or presentation must play back more than one source of audio. For example, your CD-ROM could play back digital audio through an internal speaker or via a speaker jack, but the CD-ROM could also playback regular CD audio through the CD player. To hear both sound sources, you'll need to have some device to mix them.

Audio playback cards, speakers, and CD-ROM drives are just three parts of a multimedia system. So beware of vendors who insist that their multimedia package contains everything you need to create or play back your titles. You'll still need to install the right graphics and digital video and system software, as well as configure your system hardware. Chances are that your "multimedia" audio package will add high-quality sound and access to CD-ROM material, but little else to your personal computer system.

Typical Audio Playback Systems

Each multimedia system varies in how it plays back audio from within its system. However, this model is common among most computer-based multimedia systems, especially what you might find in home playback systems.

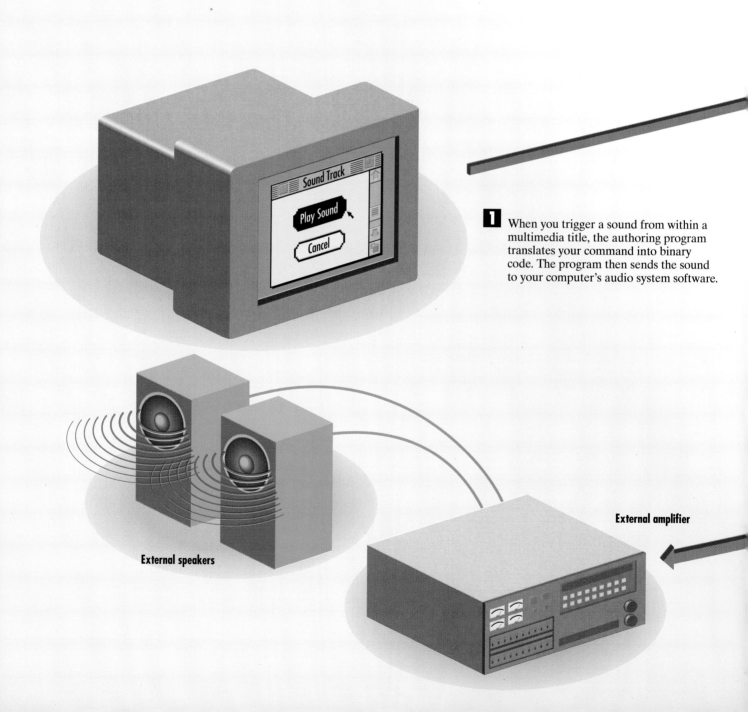

1 When you trigger a sound from within a multimedia title, the authoring program translates your command into binary code. The program then sends the sound to your computer's audio system software.

External amplifier

External speakers

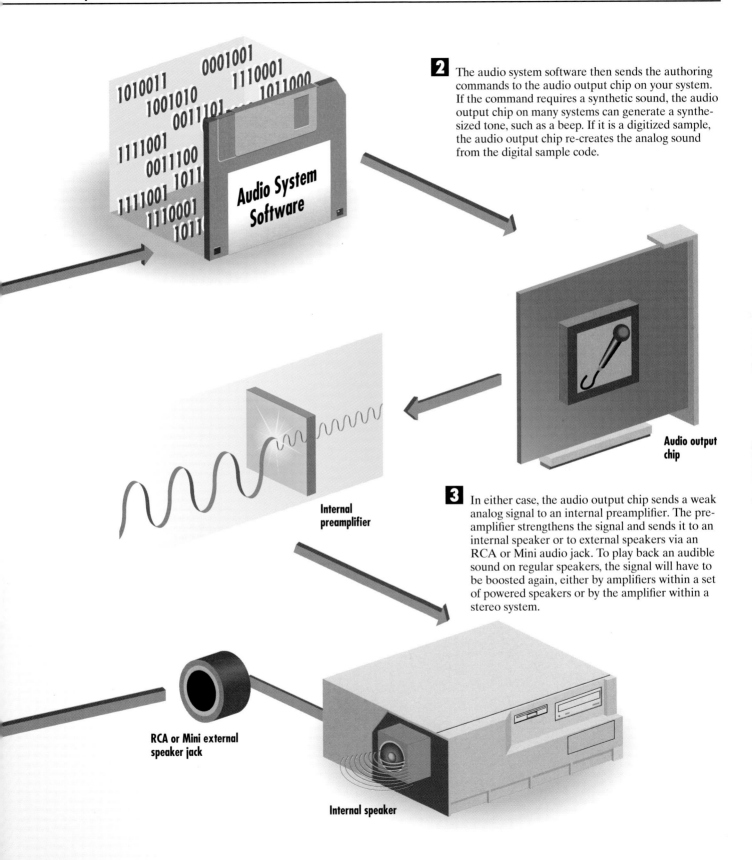

2 The audio system software then sends the authoring commands to the audio output chip on your system. If the command requires a synthetic sound, the audio output chip on many systems can generate a synthesized tone, such as a beep. If it is a digitized sample, the audio output chip re-creates the analog sound from the digital sample code.

Audio System
Software

Audio output
chip

Internal
preamplifier

3 In either case, the audio output chip sends a weak analog signal to an internal preamplifier. The preamplifier strengthens the signal and sends it to an internal speaker or to external speakers via an RCA or Mini audio jack. To play back an audible sound on regular speakers, the signal will have to be boosted again, either by amplifiers within a set of powered speakers or by the amplifier within a stereo system.

RCA or Mini external
speaker jack

Internal speaker

Understanding MIDI

MIDI, MUSICAL INSTRUMENT Digital Interface, is a communications standard that electronic musical equipment vendors created. It defines how computer music programs, synthesizers, and other electronic equipment can exchange both information and electrical signals.

While MIDI is an important part of multimedia audio production, it is not a digital audio technology. Think of it this way: If digital audio were a tape recording of a person playing a guitar solo, MIDI would be the sheet music for that same solo. While sheet music itself doesn't generate any actual sound, it does define how fast the music is played, which notes are plucked, and how loudly the guitar is strummed.

MIDI was created initially to resolve hardware incompatibilities between different electronic music instruments. In the 1970s, the different synthesizer brands couldn't talk to each other because each model had its own proprietary electronics system. There was no practical way to hook them up so that you could play two or more synthesizers from one keyboard. In August 1983, the MIDI 1.0 specification was released to remedy this problem.

MIDI 1.0 basically defined a way for different synthesizers to talk to each other using a standard type of data and a universal cable system. In this way, a musician could play one keyboard but have it control many different synthesizers at one time. This was a major breakthrough in standardization and cooperation between competing music vendors, and today virtually every electronic instrument—from department store keyboards to professional digital synthesizers—is a MIDI instrument.

The most important link that MIDI creates is the one between a personal computer and synthesizers. A computer can use a translator called a *MIDI interface* to save and manipulate MIDI data, which is binary. When the MIDI instrument receives the new MIDI data from the computer, the instrument plays it back exactly the same way it was put into the computer. This is a major boon for musicians, composers, and sound designers, who use MIDI music systems for a variety of production tasks. Whether they need to quickly create and test entire orchestral scores or create complex sound designs without the need for expensive recording equipment, MIDI is a major part of their production setup.

How MIDI Hardware Works

There are numerous MIDI setups for multimedia production: However, a basic MIDI setup would look something like this. A synthesizer is connected via MIDI to a computer. The computer sends MIDI data via a MIDI interface to other external devices. When the computer sends MIDI data back to the synthesizer and external devices, those devices generate data. The output of the MIDI instruments is sent through an audio mixer, amplified, and then sent out through speakers.

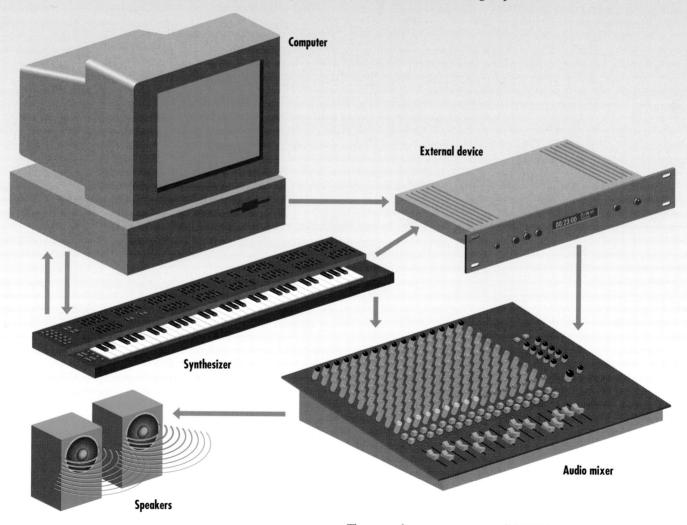

Computer

External device

Synthesizer

Audio mixer

Speakers

MIDI In **MIDI Out** **MIDI Thru**

The ports that are common to all MIDI instruments are MIDI In, MIDI Out, and MIDI Thru. They are the gateways for devices to talk to each other. These ports use a 5-pin DIN or MIDI cable instead of regular audio cables so one cable can both send and receive MIDI data.

When you play a MIDI keyboard, the electrical signals that define how you played a set of notes are sent to a built-in MIDI microprocessor chip. This MIDI processing chip converts the data into a binary data stream, and sends it to the MIDI output port. When data comes in, the process is reversed. The MIDI processing chip changes the binary data stream from the MIDI input into electrical signals that the synthesizer can use to define how a sound should be played.

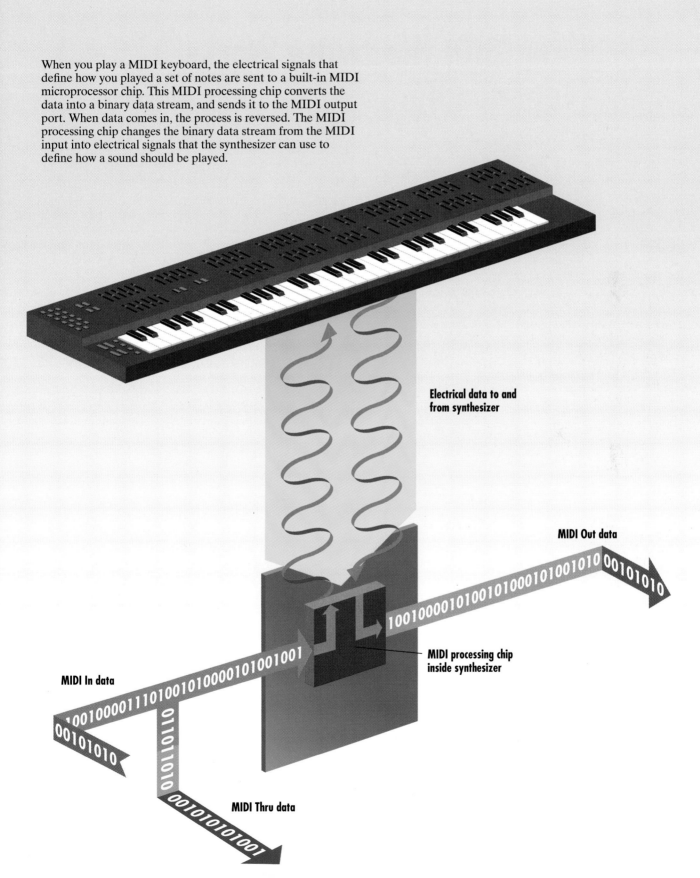

Electrical data to and from synthesizer

MIDI Out data

MIDI processing chip inside synthesizer

MIDI In data

MIDI Thru data

How MIDI Hardware Works (Continued)

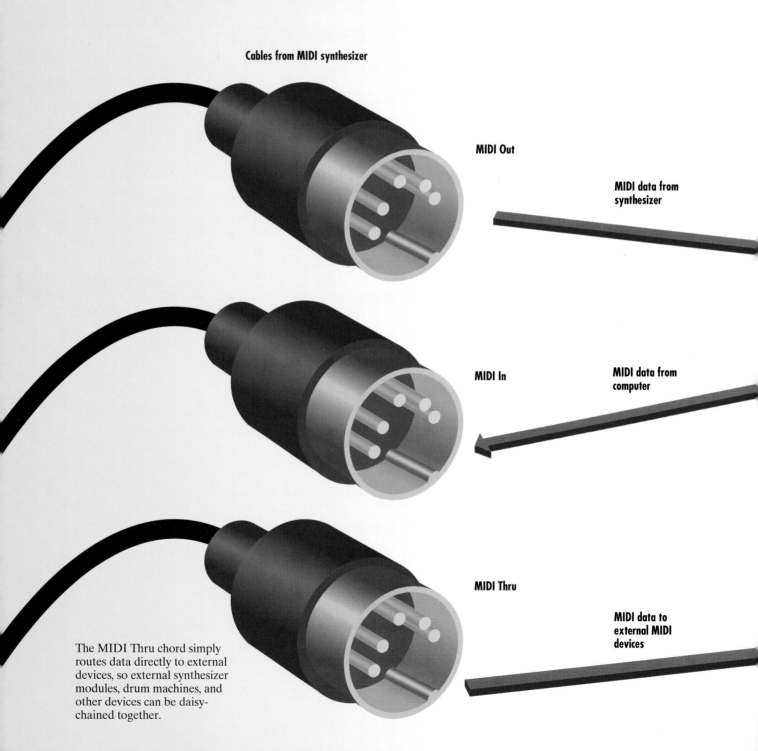

Cables from MIDI synthesizer

MIDI Out

MIDI data from synthesizer

MIDI In

MIDI data from computer

MIDI Thru

MIDI data to external MIDI devices

The MIDI Thru chord simply routes data directly to external devices, so external synthesizer modules, drum machines, and other devices can be daisy-chained together.

The MIDI data from the 5-pin MIDI cables must be sent to a MIDI interface before it can be sent to the computer. The MIDI interface takes the binary MIDI data from two of the pins on the keyboard's MIDI Out cable. The MIDI interface then sends MIDI data to the computer via a serial cable, which is usually hooked up to the modem or printer port on a computer. After manipulating data, the computer sends the data back through the serial cable to the MIDI interface. The processed MIDI data is then sent back to the synthesizer from the MIDI interface using the keyboard's MIDI In cable.

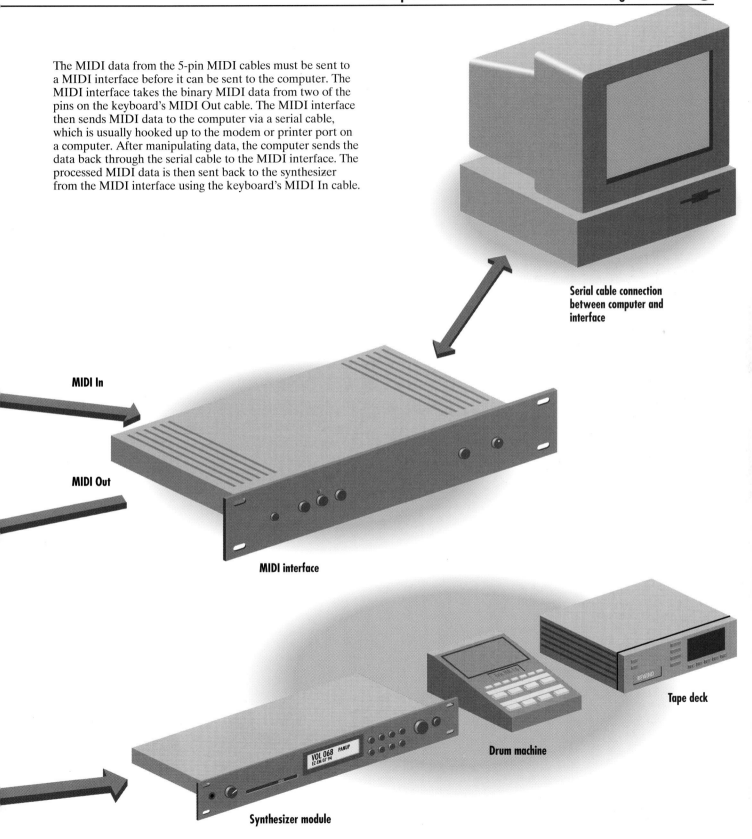

Serial cable connection between computer and interface

MIDI In

MIDI Out

MIDI interface

Synthesizer module

Drum machine

Tape deck

How MIDI Software Works

The beauty of MIDI is that it can send many messages at once. For example, when you hit a chord on a keyboard, you not only send the information of what notes you hit, but also how hard you hit the keys, how fast you played them, if you held down the damper pedal at the same time, and many other pieces of information.

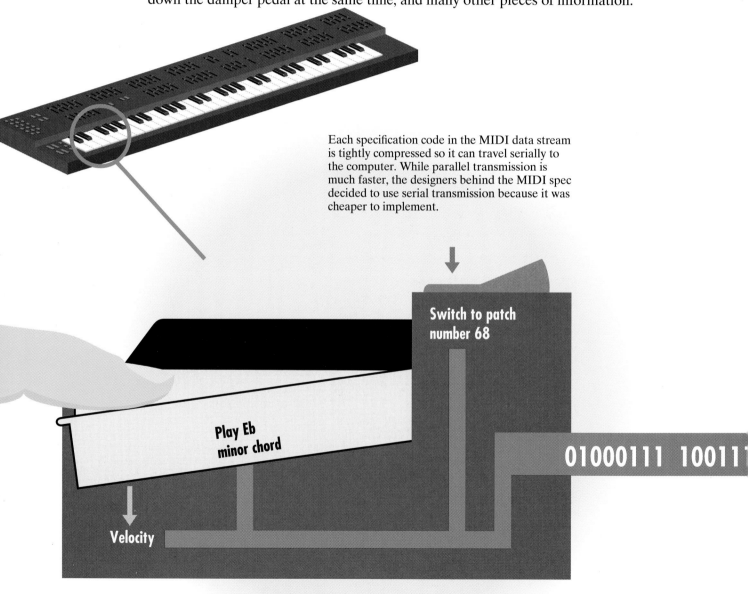

Each specification code in the MIDI data stream is tightly compressed so it can travel serially to the computer. While parallel transmission is much faster, the designers behind the MIDI spec decided to use serial transmission because it was cheaper to implement.

Switch to patch number 68

Play Eb minor chord

Velocity

01000111 10011

At the computer, the serial data stream is reassembled into MIDI commands that the computer can record, change, and manipulate. Because you can send so much information, your machine can occasionally get flooded with too much data. This can be fixed with more sophisticated MIDI hardware.

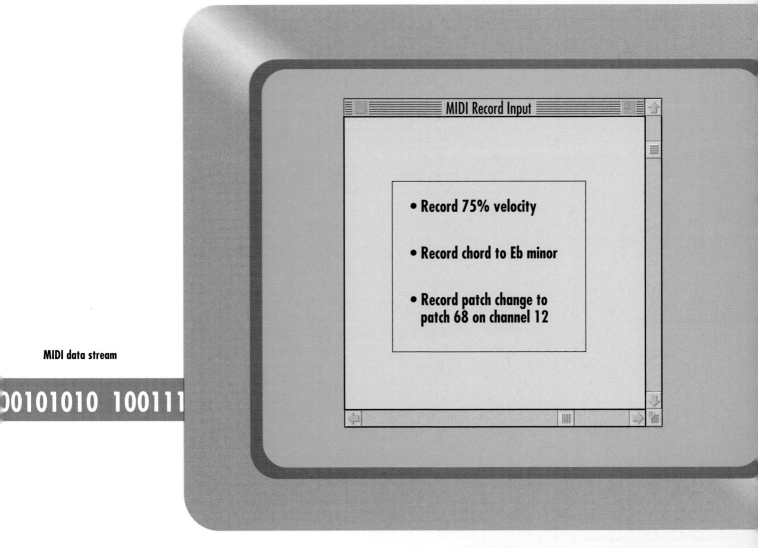

MIDI data stream

00101010 100111

To properly decode the serial MIDI code, a MIDI command or byte is wedged in by a start and stop bit at the beginning and end of the byte. These start and stop bits are discarded by the MIDI interface as each command is reassembled.

MIDI data byte

Start and stop bits

6
ALTERNATE DISTRIBUTION PLATFORMS

C O N T E N T S

TOO OFTEN WHEN you hear talk of multimedia, home video games and personal computers seem like the only ways to distribute multimedia titles. In reality, these are only two ways that producers can bring multimedia to the general public. Public access kiosks, multimedia networks, and virtual reality (VR) systems are three other multimedia distribution platforms that could have even more impact than home entertainment systems. While these systems may seem a little obscure, they could ultimately be responsible for popularizing multimedia with the general public.

Take public access kiosks, for example: While most folks may know little about typical computer multimedia playback systems, chances are they are very familiar with kiosks. Kiosks are interactive systems that combine sound, graphics, and video. You've probably seen kiosks everywhere from shopping malls to airports to retail stores. Kiosks are those "TVs" with screens you can touch to get directions in airports, create custom versions of sheet music, or even buy lottery tickets. Automated Teller Machines (ATMs) are the most primitive of all kiosks. As the technology improves, you could even see ATMS use multimedia to provide new services and perhaps an improved user interface.

Multimedia networks are the next big trend in distribution; they're in the news quite often. You've even heard members of the current presidential administration talk about multimedia networks; only when they talk about it, they call it the "information super-highway" or the National Information Infrastructure (NII). If you think these terms only refer to electronic mail and other standard text-based computing systems, think again.

Cable companies and phone companies across the country are scrambling to provide home-based multimedia services. Once the dust clears from the cable television/ phone company merger feeding frenzy, you can bet there will be a host of new services that will make simplistic services like pay-per-view pale by comparison.

Virtual reality systems use computers, a variety of hardware control systems, and customized hardware to create a 3-D world that you can explore as though it really exists. The holodeck on "Star Trek: The Next Generation" is the ultimate example of how you might one day use VR. In the holodeck, you use a massively powerful computer to create any desired setting or location with breathtaking clarity and realism. While a VR system is the least available multimedia distribution platform, it could also be the most compelling.

Even though we are many decades away from the holodeck level of VR technology, less sophisticated but powerful VR systems are being developed quite rapidly. You might not see the holodeck for quite some time, but you can count on VR technologies to inevitably change the way we experience any media.

Of course, as with most areas of multimedia, the success of these alternate distribution platforms is anyone's guess. However, consider this: None of these distribution platforms or services makes users feel like they are using a personal computer. This may seem like a trivial point, yet by taking the computer out of the equation, you bring the intimidation factor way down and open your audience up to trying out what appears to be a new type of TV.

In the future, you may be able to just pick up a remote control or touch a button on a television screen instead of learning how to use a computer's operating system. Ultimately, the reduced learning curve and ease of use of these systems will be very popular with consumers. Any bells and whistles offered by a multimedia video game machine or personal computer system could take a back seat to kiosks, VR systems, and multimedia networks.

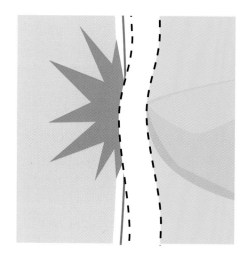

CHAPTER 20

Public Access Kiosks

KIOSKS MAY LOOK like mysterious boxes with a video screen in the middle, but they are really quite simple in construction. There are just a few main parts to a kiosk: a touch screen, a computer with a hard disk, possibly a CD-ROM player, some speakers, and a durable enclosure to house all these things. The challenge in creating kiosks is to make a system that is virtually glitch-free, so it never breaks down when used by the general public.

A touch screen is the key input device for the kiosk. A touch screen takes the place of a mouse or keyboard by allowing you to touch the video monitor's screen to make choices within the kiosk's software program. There are five different touch-screen technologies used in kiosks: capacitive, Surface Acoustic Wave (SAW), resistive membrane, infrared, and pressure sensitive. Each system uses a slightly different technology to determine where you are touching the screen. For example, resistive membrane and capacitive touch screens will find your finger by noting changes in the voltage running through the screen. On the other hand, SAW touch screens send acoustic data across the screen and analyze the changes in the sound wave.

Creating software for a touch-screen system is a very difficult task, because people have different sized hands and touch the screen in distinct ways. Consequently, you'll find that the buttons on the screen in most kiosks are quite large. This is because a touch screen can't track your finger's movements as precisely as a traditional input device, such as a computer mouse or a trackball. The larger buttons give the touch screen more latitude in determining your finger's location, and what action to trigger in the software program.

A rugged enclosure is another vital kiosk component. The enclosure has to be durable enough to withstand moving or bumping, strong enough for people to lean on, waterproof in case someone spills liquid on it, and scratch-resistant so it still looks appealing after a few months of use. As you can imagine, this is no small task, and producers generally purchase custom enclosures from companies that specialize in this type of hardware. Still, kiosks are used in dozens of business, government, and educational applications. Ultimately these kiosks will play a subtle but important role in multimedia distribution.

How a Kiosk Works

Using a kiosk is the same as using a computer to play back a multimedia title. The difference is that you use the touch screen to make your selections instead of a keyboard or a mouse.

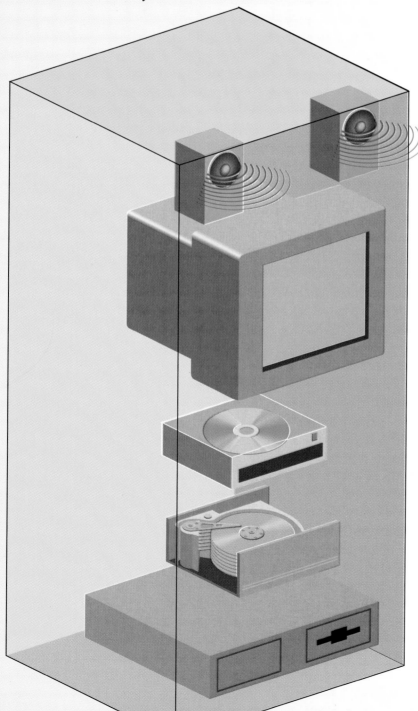

When you press on a touch screen in a kiosk, a sensor layer placed over the video screen determines where you touched the screen and notifies the computer. The computer in turn interprets this as if you had clicked on the screen with a mouse, and triggers the part of the multimedia software that corresponds to where you touched on screen.

Although a CD-ROM can be used in the system, it is generally only used as a way to update the main program on the computer's internal hard disk. With the advent of digital video technologies, more kiosks read their data off of hard disks to get the best digital video image quality.

The computer inside contains the main software program, and other hardware for outputting digital audio and video. While kiosk computers can be quite powerful, generally they are lower-end models that were purchased for their list price rather than their feature set. Given the wear and tear on a kiosk, it doesn't make sense to spend a lot of money on a high-end Mac or PC computer.

How Touch Screens Work

While there are five different touch-screen technologies available, they all work on the same principle of tracking where your finger touches the screen.

For example, in a resistive touch-screen technology screen, a rugged transparent plastic sheet is stretched over a glass plate of a monitor. The facing surfaces of the glass and plastic sheet are coated with a transparent conductive coating and kept separate. Then a low-voltage signal is sent along the face of the monitor from the touch-screen controller in the computer.

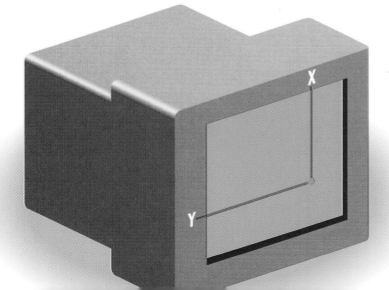

When you touch the screen, you cause the conductive coatings on the sheet and the monitor to make contact. The touch-screen controller senses the change in voltage and measures this to determine the horizontal (X) and vertical (Y) where you touched the screen.

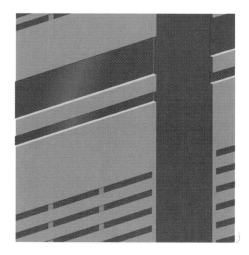

Multimedia Networks

Multimedia networks are a hot topic today, but you'll hardly ever hear that term applied to them. The *information superhighway* is the more popular term for multimedia networks, a term popularized by Vice President Al Gore. Whatever you call it, the concept of sending the digital video, animation, and data in multimedia titles over a nationwide network is an exciting prospect for producers.

A potential market of millions of subscribers encourages producers to create far more diverse and eclectic multimedia titles. So while an interactive program on how to bake French bread may be too limited for distribution on CD-ROM, it's something that could find success with the larger market on the information superhighway.

Keep in mind that the 500 channels that will be available on the information superhighway aren't all cable TV channels, but are channels that companies will reserve for sending data back and forth to you, the consumer. A video game channel may have six channels dedicated to it, so that there would be enough bandwidth to quickly send data. While this grouping of channels will limit the amount of programs available, it should ensure that you receive data fast enough for smooth game play and fast interaction.

The off-ramps that lead to your home are the major stumbling block with the information superhighway. While both cable television and telephone companies are vying to be the service that provides access to the information superhighway, neither system is currently set up to send and receive large amounts of data. The standard copper wiring that connects to most phones doesn't have much bandwidth to carry data. Fiber-optic phone cable used in high-volume transmission sites can carry much more information, but the cost of putting this into every house in the country would be extremely expensive.

More than likely your link to the information superhighway will be a combination of fiber-optic, copper, coaxial cable, and possibly some other link that is currently under development. This would allow you to receive video data over the coaxial cable and information over the fiber-optic line; you could send your responses over your standard phone line.

n

How a Multimedia Network Works

Here is one potential scenario for how you might receive programming over a multimedia network. Obviously, this will change as new systems and technologies appear. Still, given the number of companies working on these systems, it's a matter of when—and not if—there will be a multimedia network for your home.

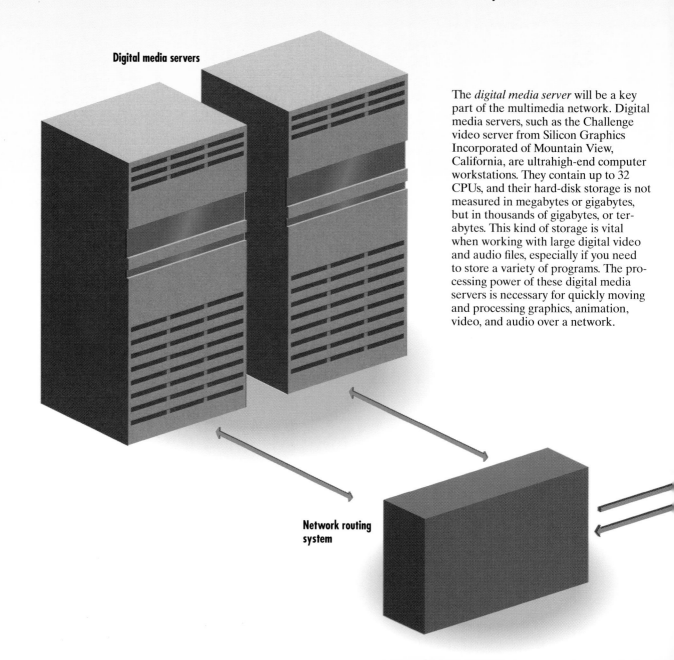

Digital media servers

The *digital media server* will be a key part of the multimedia network. Digital media servers, such as the Challenge video server from Silicon Graphics Incorporated of Mountain View, California, are ultrahigh-end computer workstations. They contain up to 32 CPUs, and their hard-disk storage is not measured in megabytes or gigabytes, but in thousands of gigabytes, or terabytes. This kind of storage is vital when working with large digital video and audio files, especially if you need to store a variety of programs. The processing power of these digital media servers is necessary for quickly moving and processing graphics, animation, video, and audio over a network.

Network routing system

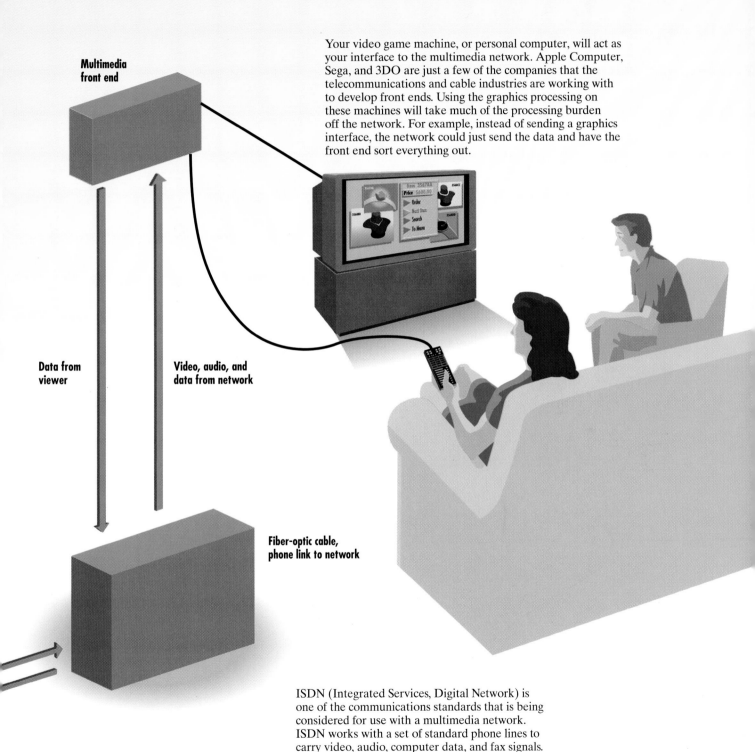

Multimedia front end

Your video game machine, or personal computer, will act as your interface to the multimedia network. Apple Computer, Sega, and 3DO are just a few of the companies that the telecommunications and cable industries are working with to develop front ends. Using the graphics processing on these machines will take much of the processing burden off the network. For example, instead of sending a graphics interface, the network could just send the data and have the front end sort everything out.

Data from viewer

Video, audio, and data from network

Fiber-optic cable, phone link to network

ISDN (Integrated Services, Digital Network) is one of the communications standards that is being considered for use with a multimedia network. ISDN works with a set of standard phone lines to carry video, audio, computer data, and fax signals. The disadvantage to ISDN is that most phone companies are not yet set up to handle it, so ISDN currently is only in the domain of big business.

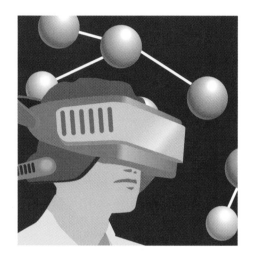

Understanding Virtual Reality

VIRTUAL REALITY (VR) is one of the most futuristic and least definable multimedia distribution platforms. When you use a VR system, it creates illusions of traveling and interacting with computer-generated images. VR systems use complex head-mounted displays, 3-D animation, and unique input devices in order to effect these illusions. Once you put on the head-mounted display, you experience a world of 3-D images: Turn your head in any direction, and the display will animate the graphics to move to that position. When you combine this particular hardware with an input device such as a data glove, joystick, or even a mouse, you have a VR system. This additional hardware gives you the ability to interact with 3-D images in this world.

So, how exactly will VR fit into multimedia? Will VR become the ultimate way we interact with multimedia titles, or just become a quirky technology that is forever "in progress"? The truth lies somewhere between the two, once you understand the limitations of a VR system. When you talk about VR, it's difficult to sort out the potential from the hype.

The film *Lawnmower Man*, is one of the most interesting and yet misleading examples of VR. The VR world portrayed in this film is beautiful. The characters fly around in a computer-generated world filled with incredible animation that responds to your every whim. However, this world was animated traditionally, one frame at a time. Current VR systems just don't have the horsepower or the data throughput to create 3-D worlds that sophisticated.

Today, the air force and NASA use the most advanced VR systems as flight simulators and testing systems, respectively. These VR systems use high-end computer workstations, specialized graphics hardware, and a full cockpit to provide incredibly realistic flight simulations. The computer workstation can create fully texture mapped 3-D graphics on two or more screens while adapting to all the pilots' commands. This level of technology won't reach the consumer for a long while, as such a VR system can cost over $300,000.

VR systems will first gain ground with the general public in the form of arcade games. There are already several firms, such as the Virtual World Centers in Boston, New York, and many other cities, that provide public access to VR games.

How a Virtual Reality System Works

Many different VR systems are under development, including high-end *total immersion* systems (where the user is completely surrounded by images and sound) as well as lower-cost *partial immersion* systems. Partial immersion systems allow the user to look at a display with special glasses while operating a simple input device. However, each system uses the same basic components: an input device, some type of display system, a high-powered computer system, and software for creating and displaying images in a virtual world.

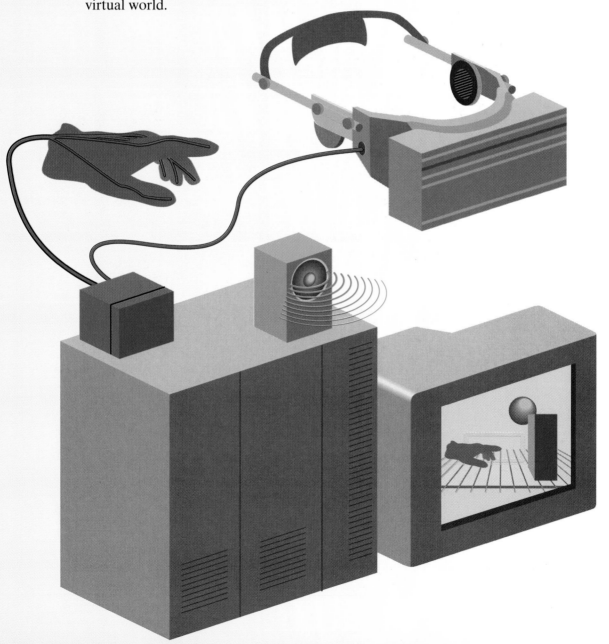

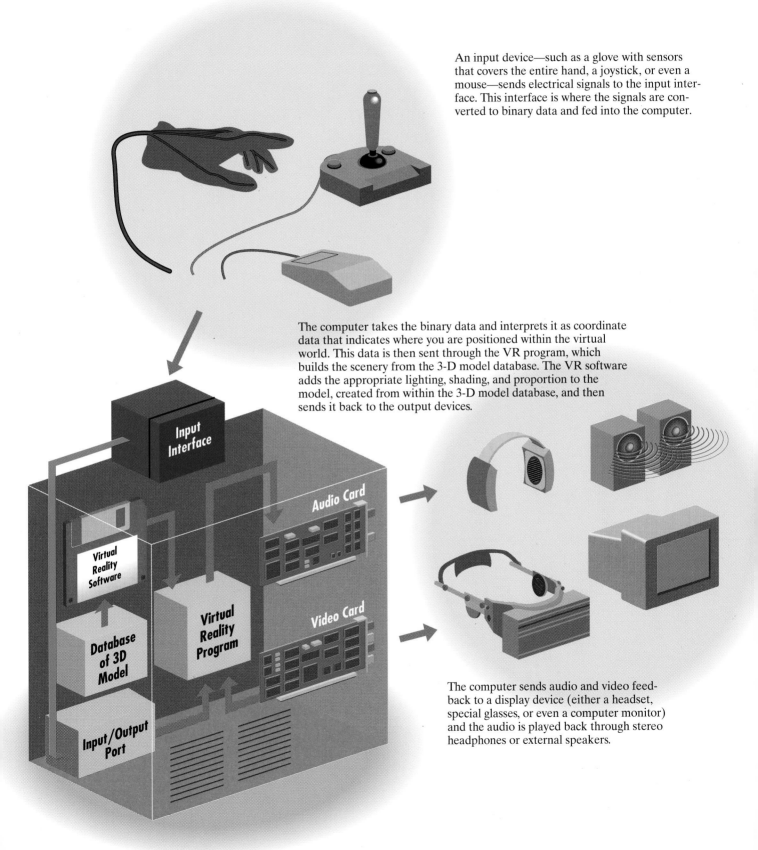

An input device—such as a glove with sensors that covers the entire hand, a joystick, or even a mouse—sends electrical signals to the input interface. This interface is where the signals are converted to binary data and fed into the computer.

The computer takes the binary data and interprets it as coordinate data that indicates where you are positioned within the virtual world. This data is then sent through the VR program, which builds the scenery from the 3-D model database. The VR software adds the appropriate lighting, shading, and proportion to the model, created from within the 3-D model database, and then sends it back to the output devices.

The computer sends audio and video feedback to a display device (either a headset, special glasses, or even a computer monitor) and the audio is played back through stereo headphones or external speakers.

Multimedia Virtual Reality Applications

While right now the cost of VR is still too high for the average consumer, eventually there will be affordable VR systems that you can hook up to some type of multimedia playback hardware. Here are a few potential VR applications, some of which are currently available.

Games

Today's VR games are generally combat simulations where you pit your skills against other players in a virtual landscape. Each player is part of a computer network that keeps track of the players' movement and score, while constantly updating graphics on each player's display system. Eventually, standard arcade games may give way to networked VR games.

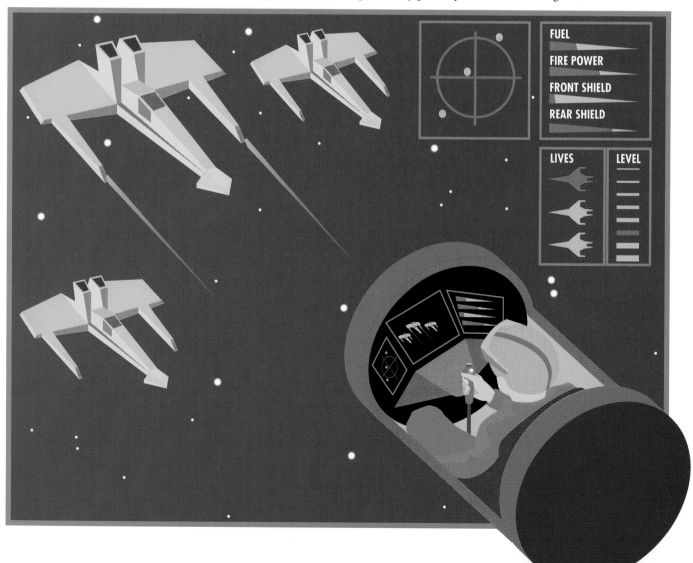

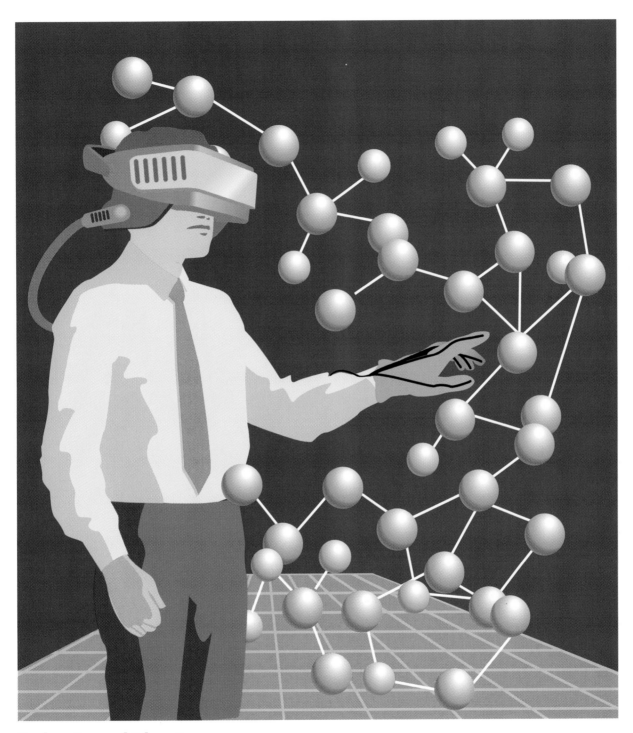

Exploration and Education

VR systems could be the next evolution of the travel show, helping you determine where you want to sightsee. Because the VR graphics are computer-generated images, it's possible to create any location—from the inside of a molecule to the top of Mount Everest. With the right 3-D database, you could also use a VR system to learn about the human body—from the inside out. Of course this requires an enormous amount of data. It will be some time before there is a personal computer or multimedia distribution system that can store, transmit, and process this kind of data fast enough to provide a realistic virtual world that changes seamlessly as you wander through it.

CD-ROMS AND
LASER DISCS

D O YOU REMEMBER record albums—those fragile vinyl discs that contained everything from your favorite rock music to songs by the heartthrob-of-the-week? It seems strange to talk about records as though they were ancient history. Yet the advent of compact discs and optical technology has moved records into the category of dated recording and playback media, which used to be reserved for gramophones, wax rolls, and player pianos. And interestingly enough, the impact that optical storage technology has had on the consumer does not end with the overwhelming acceptance of compact discs. In fact, CDs are just the beginning.

Just as record shops are going the way of the dodo bird, in just a few years you'll go to your favorite movie rental place and rent a few CDs to watch instead of VHS tapes. That's right, CD-ROM (Compact Disc Read-Only Memory) is now targeted to replace VHS video tape, that staple of today's video rental and distribution industry. CD-ROMs will eventually replace VHS videotapes just as completely as cassettes replaced 8-track tapes.

CD-ROM has an amazing amount of flexibility and potential as a multimedia storage and distribution medium. One CD-ROM can hold up to 74 minutes of digital audio or 650MB of computer data (about 464 high-density floppy disks' worth of data). Yet it costs less than $1 to duplicate a CD-ROM after you've created the glass master disc. This fact alone makes videotape distributors absolutely wide-eyed with fantasies of high profits and low overhead.

Finally, unlike records or videotapes, CD-ROM is a fairly sturdy media. Records seemed to develop scratches no matter how carefully you handled them, and your favorite videotape will inevitably sacrifice itself to your VCR. You can smudge CDs with fingerprints, drop them, even loan them to your Uncle Biff the Destroyer, and yet they'll play smoothly nearly every time. CDs are not completely indestructible, but you really have to work to destroy one.

Today there are at least four major CD standards. These standards accommodate a handful of formats for compact disc players, interactive home entertainment systems, and computer CD-ROM systems. It wasn't long after the invention of CD technology before several manufacturers brought out CD formats that could record computer data. Remember, the audio data that is recorded onto compact discs is digital binary data, the same type of data found in computer files. With a few modifications to this format of the CD, it was easy to turn audio compact disc technology into a storage medium.

While CD-ROMs store digital data on only one side of the disc, laser discs store an analog video signal on both sides of the disc. Although the video signal is analog, the quality of the video and audio on laser discs is phenomenal. Laser discs can also play back more than one channel of CD-quality audio at a time, so they are a favorite for distributing programs that contain surround-sound or a second language track. For example, on the special Criterion laser disc version of *The Seventh Voyage of Sinbad*, you can select an audio channel that contains just Bernard Herrmann's wondrous film score.

Laser discs have a long and honored place in the history of multimedia. While laser discs seemed to vanish from the public view in the mid-1980s, multimedia producers have used them for many years in kiosks and multimedia programs to hold still photographs, video, and audio. Before digital video, a laser disc was the only cost-effective way to add full-motion video to your multimedia title. Laser discs are relatively inexpensive to produce, very durable, and can be integrated with multimedia programs fairly easily.

While laser disc technology has not changed much since its introduction, it still has a place in the future of multimedia and home entertainment technology. As the move to wide-screen video technology continues, more distributors continue to use laser discs as a great storage alternative for wide-screen programming. When you combine digital video compression technology with the storage potential on a laser disc, the sky is the limit for new types of multimedia programs.

Understanding CD-ROMs

DIGITAL VIDEO, HIGH-QUALITY audio, photo-realistic graphics, and stunning animation are some of the best elements of a multimedia title...until you want to distribute it. Suddenly your three minutes of audio transforms itself into 30MB of audio files—and digital animation and video files take up even more room. Even in very conservative multimedia projects, it's not difficult to end up with a project that contains over a hundred megabytes of data. CD-ROMs offer an inexpensive solution to this problem, allowing producers to fill up a single CD-ROM with up to 650MB of data.

Still, CD-ROMs are not without shortcomings. The main problem with CD-ROMs is slow data processing speed. A regular hard disk can retrieve and send data to a computer much more quickly than a CD-ROM can. While newer hard-disk technologies can send many megabytes of data to and from a computer each second, the newest triple speed CD-ROM drives can barely deliver 450K of data per second. Even a data rate of 450K per second is blindingly fast compared to the early CD-ROM drives, which oozed data out at a blistering 150K per second.

Interestingly, instead of waiting for newer CD-ROM technology, most producers design their titles to work within the limitations of CD-ROM technology. It's quite common to adjust the playback of your digital movie files so that they will not exceed the known data rate of most CD-ROM drives. There are even programs that can simulate the access time of a CD-ROM on a hard disk, so you can see just how slowly you can expect your title to run on a CD-ROM.

The variety of CD-ROM standards can also cause problems (this is typical of most areas of multimedia). True, audio CDs and CD-ROMs are all the same size, with the same hole in the middle and a shiny metallic surface covered with clear plastic: The question is, what format is your CD-ROM? A Mac HFS CD-ROM disc is not readable on a Windows machine, while neither system can read a CD-1 or 3DO CD-ROM disc. Even worse, if you played a PhotoCD on a traditional CD audio deck, you could damage your speakers.

The solution, of course, is to pick a CD format that best fits your target audience. As a way of hedging their bets, producers also use a hybrid mode CD-ROM format that combines a Mac and Windows format on the same disc. Eventually, a CD format that is compatible with any consumer or computer CD-ROM player may become available.

How a CD Stores Information

Data is recorded onto a CD in a clockwise spiral from the center. The first track that is recorded is the *lead-in*, which contains a kind of table of contents on everything that is on the disc. Next the regular computer or digital audio data is recorded out from the center. When all the data is recorded, the CD mastering machine adds a *lead-out* track to mark the end of the CD.

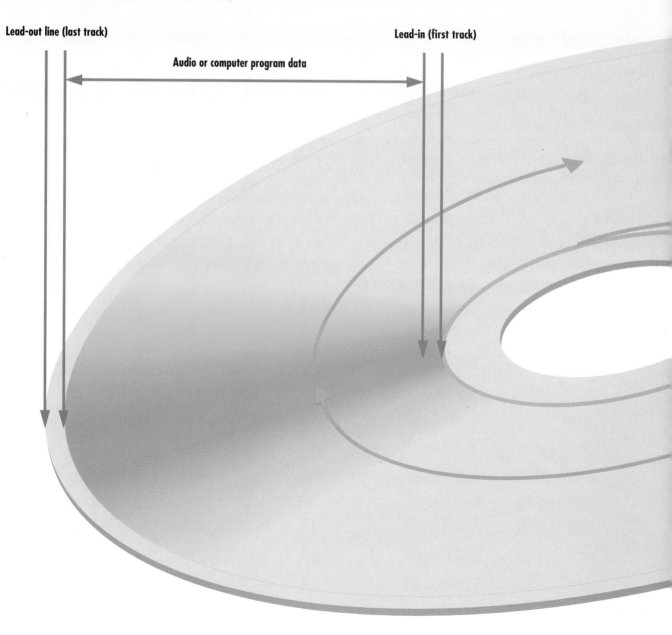

Lead-out line (last track)

Lead-in (first track)

Audio or computer program data

The CD has a reflective surface that is covered with small dents or *pits*. The reflective areas between pits are called *lands*. The laser in the CD-ROM mastering machine burns these pits into the surface. When the CD-ROM player reads the disc, the laser inside the machine moves across the surface from the center.

Any pit that the laser hits fails to reflect the laser back to the read head in the CD-ROM. When this happens, the photo sensor on the laser head registers an off signal. The dull pits and reflective lands on a CD-ROM do not represent binary code as on (1) or off (0) code. Instead they are counted in groups of 14 and then converted to a standard 8-digit data byte that your computer can read.

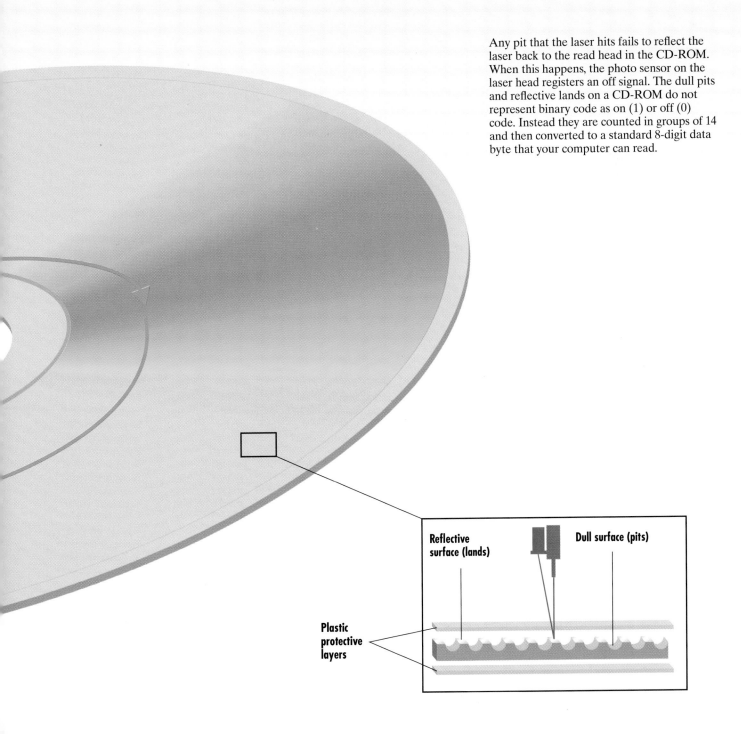

Reflective surface (lands)

Dull surface (pits)

Plastic protective layers

CD-ROM Formats

Here are the currently announced CD formats that pertain to multimedia distribution. However, the development of video games that use CD-ROMs will no doubt add a few new formats to this list.

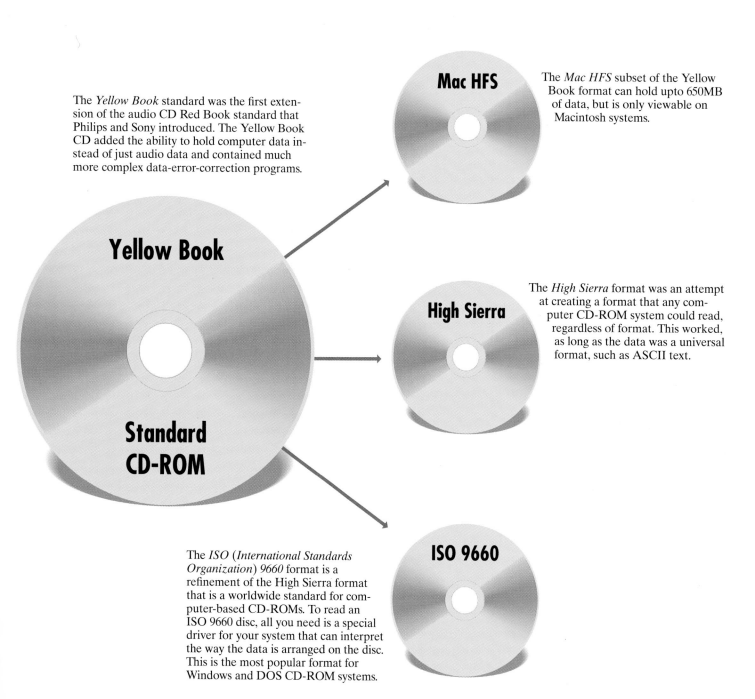

The *Yellow Book* standard was the first extension of the audio CD Red Book standard that Philips and Sony introduced. The Yellow Book CD added the ability to hold computer data instead of just audio data and contained much more complex data-error-correction programs.

Mac HFS

The *Mac HFS* subset of the Yellow Book format can hold upto 650MB of data, but is only viewable on Macintosh systems.

Yellow Book

Standard CD-ROM

High Sierra

The *High Sierra* format was an attempt at creating a format that any computer CD-ROM system could read, regardless of format. This worked, as long as the data was a universal format, such as ASCII text.

The *ISO (International Standards Organization) 9660* format is a refinement of the High Sierra format that is a worldwide standard for computer-based CD-ROMs. To read an ISO 9660 disc, all you need is a special driver for your system that can interpret the way the data is arranged on the disc. This is the most popular format for Windows and DOS CD-ROM systems.

ISO 9660

The *Red Book* standard, also referred to as CD-DA (digital/audio), was the first compact disc format that Sony and Philips created. The Red Book format defines the areas on the disc (called *tracks*) that contain audio data, as well as the error correction routines used. Today all audio compact discs are Red Book audio discs.

The *Green Book* standard is one of the first platform-specific CD-ROM formats that Sony and Philips created for *CD-I* (Compact Disc-Interactive). While this format ensures that all CD-I players can read any CD-I disc, it makes a CD-I disc unusable on any other type of CD-ROM player.

Orange Book audio is the newest format developed to define *CD-R* (Compact Disc-Recordable) systems. CD-R systems allow you to record your own data onto a CD for archiving or multimedia premastering. The main difference between the Orange Book and other formats is that you can redo the directory contained in the lead-in to show additional items that may have been added in a later recording session.

PRODUCTION NOTE Philips and Sony announced a new CD-ROM format called White Book, which is specifically for Video CD-ROMs. White Book discs can contain up to 74 minutes of MPEG digital video and audio.

How a PhotoCD Works

Kodak's PhotoCD is a unique CD-ROM format and application. The idea is simple: Instead of putting all your photographs in boxes and forgetting about them in the attic, you could store them on disc. While this process hasn't exactly caught fire with consumers, it is slowly being used in business as a way to archive photographs.

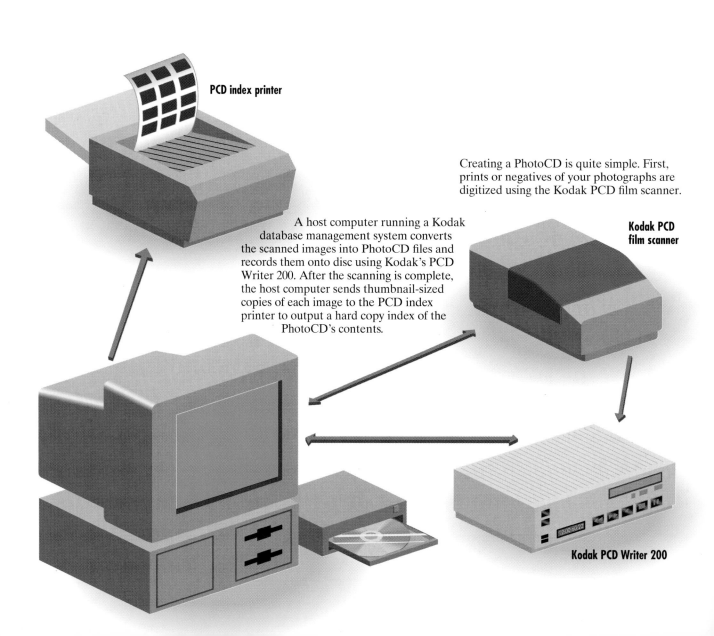

PCD index printer

Creating a PhotoCD is quite simple. First, prints or negatives of your photographs are digitized using the Kodak PCD film scanner.

A host computer running a Kodak database management system converts the scanned images into PhotoCD files and records them onto disc using Kodak's PCD Writer 200. After the scanning is complete, the host computer sends thumbnail-sized copies of each image to the PCD index printer to output a hard copy index of the PhotoCD's contents.

Kodak PCD film scanner

Kodak PCD Writer 200

1.

2.

3.

4.

5.

Each image scanned onto a PhotoCD is saved in five formats:

1. A small thumbnail image used for previewing the many files on disc.
2. A low resolution file used as an *FPO* (for placement only) file in desktop publishing and image manipulation.
3. A file with the resolution and aspect ratio adjusted so you can show the image on your television set.
4. An HDTV version of your image.
5. A superhigh resolution version of your image. This format allows you to create high quality prints that you can output from one of Kodak's thermal color printers.

**NASA file photograph
courtesy of Colorbytes, Inc.**

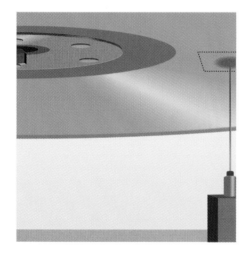

Understanding Compact Disc Recorders

COMPACT DISC RECORDABLE (CD-R) drives are the latest incarnation of *WORM* (Write Once Read Many) technology. CD-R drive systems combine several elements, including a host computer, a CD-R drive, and an external hard disk that contains the data that you plan to record. A CD-R drive uses special discs to record data onto a CD-ROM. But unlike a hard disk, you can only write to a section of a CD-R disc once because you are physically changing the surface of the disc. However, some software programs let you write additional data *after* that track. *Multisession* CD-R technology allows you to record data several times in consecutive tracks on the disc. For example, Kodak's PhotoCD lets you add more pictures to your PhotoCD in later recordings, or "sessions," on a PhotoCD CD-R disc recorder. You can play a CD-R just as though it were a CD-ROM disc.

Producers use CD-R drives as a key tool for archiving and testing. CD-R discs are just as sturdy as regular CD-ROMs, so producers use CD-R drives as a security blanket to back up critical files on their hard disks. Considering that a blank 650MB CD-R disc costs only about $20, CD-R discs offer the producer a very economical way to save the sizable sound, video, and graphics files created during the project.

Producers use CD-R discs to test the performance of the digital video and audio when it is played back from a CD-ROM drive. In fact, CD-R discs are one of the best media to use in order to accurately evaluate your multimedia title's overall performance. As I mentioned in Chapter 12, the data rates on a CD-ROM drive are not nearly as fast as those on a hard disk, so it's important to limit the data playback rate of digital audio and video files.

You can record a wide variety of data on CD-R discs, from Red Book CD-audio discs to Yellow Book computer CD-ROMs to Green Book CD-I discs. The only formats that CD-R recorders can't accommodate are the proprietary video CD-ROM formats from Sega, Nintendo, and other video game hardware manufacturers.

How Recordable CD-ROM Drives Work

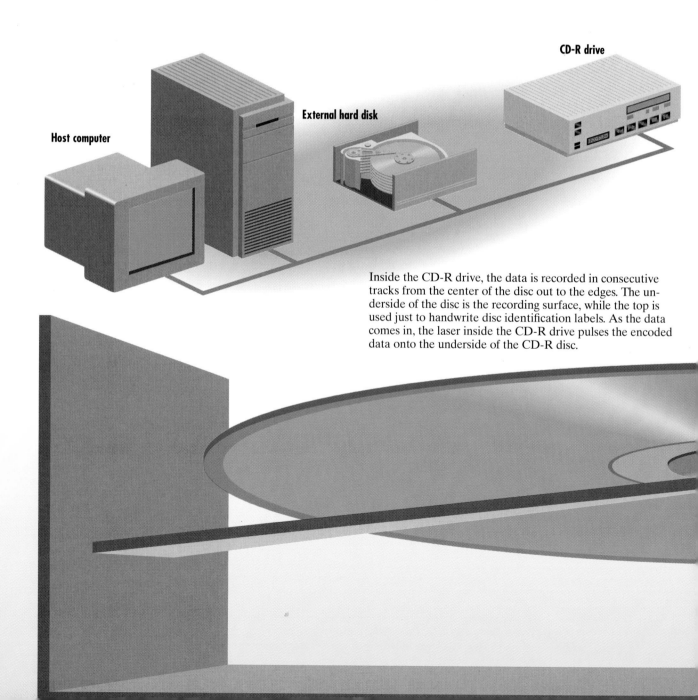

CD-R drive

External hard disk

Host computer

Inside the CD-R drive, the data is recorded in consecutive tracks from the center of the disc out to the edges. The underside of the disc is the recording surface, while the top is used just to handwrite disc identification labels. As the data comes in, the laser inside the CD-R drive pulses the encoded data onto the underside of the CD-R disc.

The CD-R disc adds several layers to the conventional CD-ROM format. The first layer is a clear plastic that protects the surface. Next a layer of green photosensitive dye is melded with a gold metallic reflective layer. Finally all the layers are melded over a pre-grooved surface. As the laser light hits the surface of the disc, it erodes the dye to form the same surface found in regular CD-ROM discs.

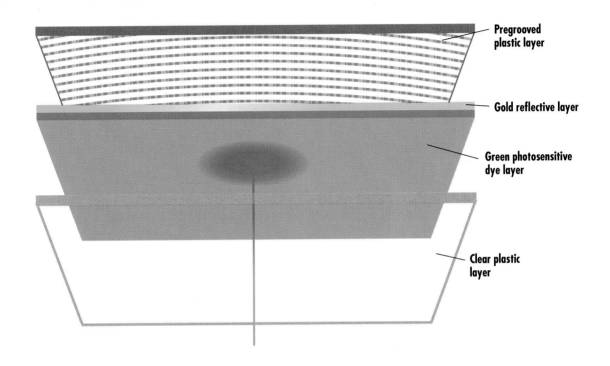

Pregrooved plastic layer

Gold reflective layer

Green photosensitive dye layer

Clear plastic layer

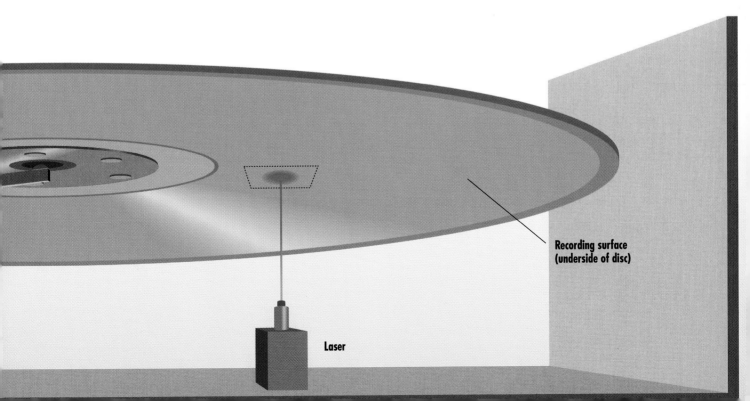

Recording surface (underside of disc)

Laser

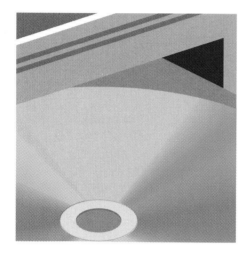

Understanding Laser Discs

A LASER DISC LOOKS like a large CD-ROM and it is the size and shape of a 12-inch album. Both use similar types of recording media, and like a CD, a laser disc can record and play back high quality digital audio files. However, laser discs can play back four audio channels at a time (two digital audio channels and two analog), compared to the two audio channels of a CD.

Despite the similarities between laser discs and CDs, there are vast differences between the two. The biggest difference is laser discs store video in analog signals. Unlike compact discs or CD-ROMs, the analog signal on a laser disc player is not converted to a digital signal and then sent through an analog-to-digital converter. The signal is recorded as analog and stays analog when it is sent to your television set, which is why laser discs provide the best video quality that you can get on a consumer video playback system.

The disadvantage to using laser discs is you can't work with video as though it were a digital video file. This means you can't work with it at the software level, because the analog output of a laser disc is just like any other video source. You can digitize the laser-disc video, but this results in lower quality images and fewer audio channels.

Multimedia producers have long used laser discs as a way to add full-motion video to their titles. Before digital video came along, the only other way to add video to your title was to trigger an expensive video deck from the host computer. Not only was this not cost-effective, but the constant shuttling back and forth also wreaked havoc on the source material; eventually, the wear and tear would destroy the videotape.

Laser discs are still a cheap way to incorporate full-motion, full-screen video into a multimedia title. A Write Once Read Many (WORM) laser disc costs about $300, and the most expensive laser disc players still cost less than $1,500. You can create full-motion video using digital video technology, but you have to invest in expensive hardware to play it back. Since the cost of a full-screen digital video card and the required hard-disk storage can cost at least $6,000, laser discs continue to be a useful tool for multimedia presentations and titles.

Laser Disc Formats

Standard laser discs that you rent or buy at a store come in two formats: CAV (Constant Angular Velocity) and CLV (Constant Linear Velocity). Which format you use depends upon how much video you need to store and how you plan to access the laser disc material.

CAV (Constant Angular Velocity)

CAV is the laser disc format of choice for most multimedia projects. The disc rotates at a fixed speed of 1,800 RPM, so it plays at the same speed no matter where the read head is on the laser disc. Because a CAV laser disc uses many concentric tracks, every frame and every section of video is uniquely addressable. This is vital in multimedia titles, where different events must trigger specific images or video. The downside to the CAV format is it can only hold 30 minutes of video or 54,000 still frames per side. Since it takes a few minutes to turn the laser disc over, in multimedia presentations most producers just pack one side of a disc. If they need to address more than 30 minutes of material, most producers will use several laser disc players synchronized by one computer for control to maintain playback speed and continuity.

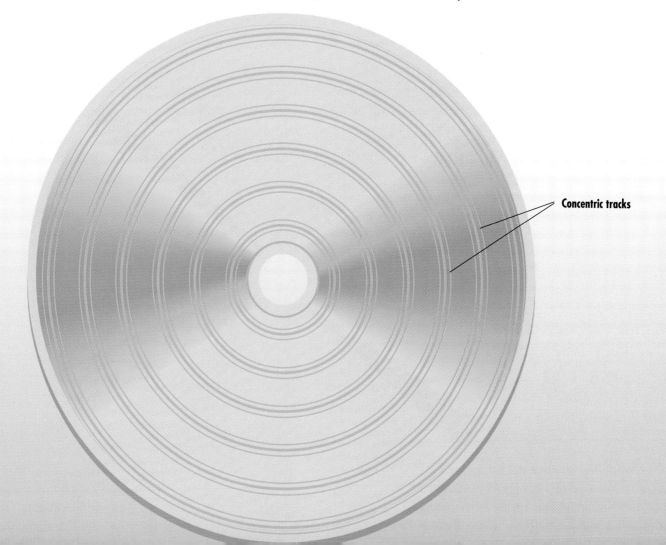

Concentric tracks

CLV (Constant Linear Velocity)

CLV uses a single spiral track starting at the center that circles out to the edge, like a record album. The laser disc player keeps the playback speed constant by changing the speed at which the disc revolves: The player slows down when the read head is near the center, but speeds up when the read head is at the edge of the disc. The main advantage to using CLV discs is they can hold 60 minutes of video per side, so you can store a two-hour program on a single disc. However, you can't display still frames on CLV discs unless you use special hardware. You also miss out on a few other operating features common with CAV discs, such as the ability to move through a program frame-by-frame, or to search to a specific frame on the disc.

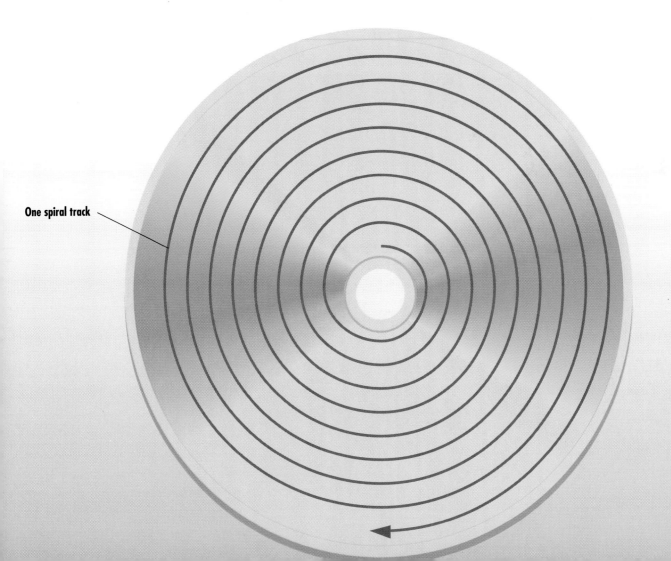

One spiral track

Laser Disc Application Levels

Multimedia producers refer to one of three levels when describing how they've integrated laser discs into a presentation or a title. Set many years ago, these levels still apply to the ways in which laser discs are used in multimedia.

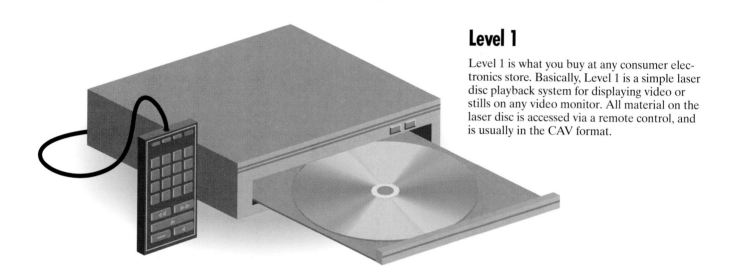

Level 1

Level 1 is what you buy at any consumer electronics store. Basically, Level 1 is a simple laser disc playback system for displaying video or stills on any video monitor. All material on the laser disc is accessed via a remote control, and is usually in the CAV format.

Level 2

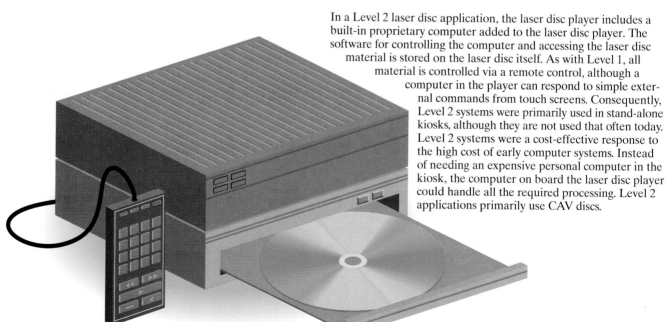

In a Level 2 laser disc application, the laser disc player includes a built-in proprietary computer added to the laser disc player. The software for controlling the computer and accessing the laser disc material is stored on the laser disc itself. As with Level 1, all material is controlled via a remote control, although a computer in the player can respond to simple external commands from touch screens. Consequently, Level 2 systems were primarily used in stand-alone kiosks, although they are not used that often today. Level 2 systems were a cost-effective response to the high cost of early computer systems. Instead of needing an expensive personal computer in the kiosk, the computer on board the laser disc player could handle all the required processing. Level 2 applications primarily use CAV discs.

PRODCUTION NOTE Bar-code readers and laser disc players are a popular combination with multimedia producers because they offer a fast way to input commands to the laser disc player. For example, instead of having to frantically push the right sequence of buttons to have the laser disc player find and then stop after playing frame 32021, you could just wave a bar-code reader over the same command in bar-code form. This is a great benefit for public speakers who want to show clips from a laser disc player, but don't have the time during their show to mess with a remote control.

Level 3

Level 3 is the highest level of laser disc applications. A laser disc player is connected and controlled via a serial port to an external computer. The computer is used to control the player and access all material on the laser disc. Often producers will provide control over the material within the multimedia title that they create. For example, clicking on an icon that said "film clip" could send a signal to the laser disc to search for a specific track, start that video segment, and then stop playing when that segment is over. Level 3 applications primarily use CAV discs.

INTERACTIVE ENTERTAINMENT

CONTENTS

NTERACTIVE ENTERTAINMENT IS one of the many terms that producers use to categorize multimedia products in developing their titles as video game systems. In many ways, home video game systems could be the ultimate multimedia distribution medium.

For some this will be a hard concept to accept. After all, some people say that video games are nothing more than the power tool of adolescent males, who maniacally seek pleasure by expressing their thirst for violence in the single-minded destruction of whole legions of space invaders. Others say that video games are this generation's way of acquiring control and status. Still others venture that video games are people's way of dealing with the many frustrating elements of their lives. Face it—whether you are 14 or 40, sometimes it's nice to sit down to a bit of heroic, escapist fun and blast the living daylights out of any electronic beastie that has the misfortune to challenge your skill.

However you feel, video games mean two things to multimedia producers and distributors: money and huge distribution potential. In fact, some of the more popular game titles have grossed hundreds of millions of dollars. Further, the millions of personal computer systems sold over the last few years is incredibly small when compared to the video game market. With a potential market measured in the millions instead of hundreds of thousands of units, multimedia producers have a better chance of recouping their production costs on a video game title than on a computer-based CD-ROM project.

Yet while newspapers and magazines often talk about the overwhelming success of Nintendo, Sega, and other home video game manufacturers, this was not always the case. After a phenomenal growth spurt that started when the home version of Atari's Pong arcade game hit in 1975, the bottom had fallen out of the video game market by 1982. Retailers were hurt by rapid obsolescence of game hardware, while many folks felt that the quality of the games available was too poor to bother with. So what spurred the video game comeback into the consumer marketplace?

Many business books have pondered the question, looking towards development costs and other business problems to explain this early slump. I believe the answer is much simpler—good software. While many things factor into the market's success, popular software titles are the most important element in the success of the video game industry.

You may not remember the names of the numerous game systems that came out over the last decade, but chances are you do remember the games themselves. From Atari's Pong or Pac Man to Nintendo's Mario Brothers, Sega's Sonic the Hedgehog, or Acclaim's Mortal Kombat—all these hit games have redefined the market, bolstered video game hardware sales, and generated profits that rival even Hollywood blockbuster films. Regardless of whether you enjoy them, the bottom line is that the market success of these titles has directly affected the strength of the video game industry and the popularity of each new video game system. Sega's success in the video game market was so tied to their Sonic the Hedgehog video game that Sonic even appeared on the company's paychecks!

Many interactive entertainment systems are available today, but they are incompatible with earlier systems. However, each new offering boasts better graphics than its predecessors. When you consider the six CD-based systems that combine video game technology with the storage muscle of CD-ROM, it's easy to understand why quite a few vendors are vying for this market. Again, a smash title on any particular platform will do more for its acceptance than any hardware specifications. As more hardware vendors incorporate computer technology into their game systems, you can look forward to home video game systems that will combine the sophistication of computer-based multimedia titles with low-cost consumer hardware.

PART EIGHT

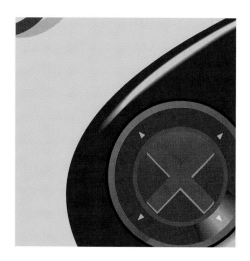

How Video Games Work

V IDEO GAME SYSTEMS are really just small, specialized computers designed for playing back animation quickly. While the hardware on these systems is limited compared to traditional computers, video game systems excel at playing animation faster than even the most powerful personal computers. This is because video games use several animation processors in conjunction with a fairly low-powered microprocessor—most personal computer systems have to process everything through one central processing unit (CPU). A video encoder is built in, so each system can output the game's computer graphics directly to your television set.

Unfortunately, there are few additional details available on the inner workings of the various machines. As you can imagine, with billions of dollars at stake, game manufacturers are somewhat reluctant to divulge trade secrets; consequently, the hardware tends to remain a mystery except to developers.

However, we can clear up one of the confusing things about video games, which occurs when vendors start talking about 8-, 16-, 32-, and even 64-bit video game systems. These "bits" ratings have to do with the processing, data throughput, and graphics capabilities of the video game system. Think of it this way: Each higher bit level is the equivalent of moving to a new generation of personal computer.

Nintendo and Sega are currently the big leaders in the cartridge video game market, with others running a somewhat distant third in the United States. Nintendo has the longest tenure, having brought out the 8-bit NES (Nintendo Entertainment System) in 1983, which was followed shortly by Sega's Genesis Master System and NEC's TurboGrafx. However, tenure doesn't necessarily equal market dominance. The greater volume of Sega games available on the market has evened the balance between Sega and Nintendo, and forced some healthy competition between the two.

While 16-bit systems seem to be the flavor of the month in home video game systems, several 64-bit systems are on the horizon. The first one to come out is the 64-bit Jaguar, the first game system from Atari in many years. Following on its heels are announcements from Sega, Nintendo, TTI, and NEC that promise to do everything that their competitors do, only better. Yet the race for the leading 64-bit machine has less to do with improving game quality than trying to capture market share.

Many cable and telecommunications companies are testing video game systems as the hardware interface for interactive television. The faster processing, data throughput, and improved graphics on the new 64-bit machines could be key in managing data on a multimedia network and appealing to consumers.

How a Sega Genesis System Works

While each 16-bit video game system deals with graphics and processing a little differently, the Sega Genesis system is a good representation of the current technology in today's 16-bit video game systems.

The main program for the video game is stored in read-only memory (ROM) on the game cartridge. These lightweight cartridges can contain 2MB or more of data. For example, the Eternal Champions game cartridge holds over 24MB of data.

PRODUCTION NOTE Sega has already announced the release of "The Saturn" in Japan, kicking off the third generation of computer games with a new game system with at least two 32-bit RISC processors. According to analysts, a Japanese announcement for Sega usually means that the United States will see the product in six months or so. While very little data was available on it when we went to press, you can count on Sega adding even more processing power and better graphics to the new system.

When you insert the cartridge into the machine, data from the ROM goes directly into the 8 MHz Motorola 68000 CPU on board the Genesis. The Genesis system contains only 64K of RAM (random-access memory) and 64K of VRAM (video random-access memory), which is infinitesimal compared to the most basic models of personal computers. However, the Genesis system also contains special sprite processors, which handle the animation of the on-screen characters. These sprite processors make sure your favorite video game character zooms along at breakneck speed.

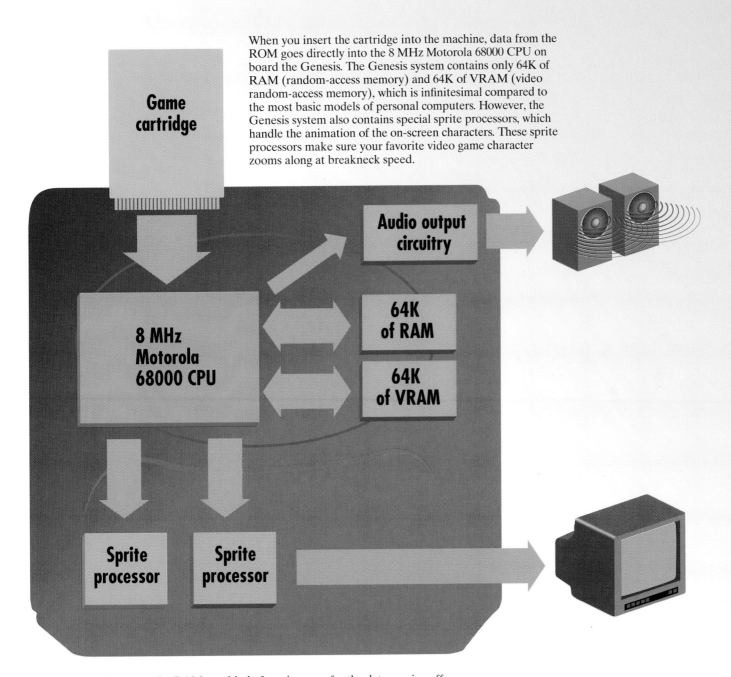

The CPU uses the RAM as a kind of staging area for the data coming off the game cartridge. The CPU constantly coordinates the sound and graphics data coming from the ROM, as well as the data coming from your game controller. Each time you press a button on your game controller, the CPU pulls the appropriate data off the ROM, arranges it in RAM, and then sends it out through the video encoder chip so you can play the game on your TV set.

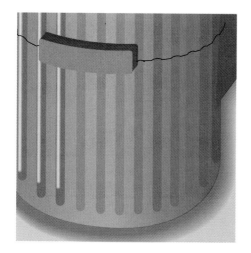

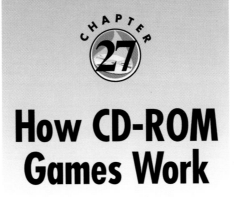

How CD-ROM Games Work

WHILE VIDEO GAMES are already working towards the third generation of technology, CD-ROM games are really still in their infancy. Part of this is due to the smattering of titles available, but mostly it is a problem of integrating CD-ROM technology into a game system.

Data throughput is one of the biggest challenges with using CD-ROMs in game systems. Most of the game cartridges use a special "burst" data transfer mode, so a great deal of data—sometimes megabytes per second—is sent to the system's CPU as needed. However, the first CD-ROM drives could barely trickle data out at 150K per second, which would drastically affect the quality of multimedia titles. Trying to access data from the CD during a game was the functional equivalent of trying to quickly drain a lake with a small straw.

However, most new systems work around this problem with custom hardware and faster CD-ROM drives. Double-speed CD-ROM drives are now standard equipment on these systems, while additional RAM acts as a storage buffer so the system can get at more data as needed.

Currently there are four CD-based systems on the U.S. home market: the Sega Genesis CD, the TTI Turbo Duo, the 3DO Interactive Multiplayer, and the Philips CD-I (Compact Disc-Interactive). Naturally, there are many upgrades and new products on the way. Several 64-bit systems—the Jaguar from Atari, Sega's Saturn, and others from NEC and Nintendo—will have a CD-ROM add-on, as well as a host of new games. Commodore, the makers of the Amiga computer, has announced a 32-bit CD-based system called the CD-32. This unit has been selling like hotcakes in Europe, but is just now reaching the United States. Experts wonder if Commodore can make a comeback after the failure of their initial CD product, the ill-fated CDTV—only time and the market will tell.

Still, the future for CD-based game systems is particularly bright, especially as a video playback system. Nearly every CD-based consumer vendor has announced support for MPEG video playback hardware as low-cost add-ons to their systems. The Video CD MPEG format endorsed by Sony, Philips, and other vendors stores up to 74 minutes of VHS-quality video on just one disc. As this video storage capability improves, it's possible that CD-based game systems will be the video playback systems of the '90s.

How 3DO Games Work

The 3DO Interactive Multiplayer from Panasonic, AT&T, Sanyo, Samsung, and GoldStar were the first CD-players to come out that showed the potential of the second generation CD-ROM home entertainment systems. While the initial titles are geared more towards the traditional video game crowd, the 3DO machine is actually more powerful than many personal computer systems.

1 Data intially comes from the double-speed CD-ROM drive and/or the game controller and goes directly into the *direct memory access* (*DMA*) controller. The DMA controller coordinates the flow of traffic through 24 separate DMA channels to the two graphics chips and one RISC (Reduced Instruction Set Computing) CPU chip. These separate DMA channels are high-band width communication paths that pass data to and from the internal components at blazing speeds. The 32-bit RISC chip is similar to the same high-speed RISC chip used in the PowerMac and PowerPC computers from Apple and IBM, respectively.

4 An MPEG decompression hardware card, additional drives, or other future peripherals will slot into the two expansion buses. The 3DO Video CD adapter plugs into the AV expansion slot on the side of the unit. This leaves the general expansion slot free for other peripherals such as the memory card reader, which gives you removable storage capabilities. Also, the voice-over data modem from AT&T is a telecommunications device that allows you to connect two 3DO systems over a standard phone line. This makes it possible to engage in two-player games over the phone while simultaneously being able to carry on a voice conversation over the same single-phone line.

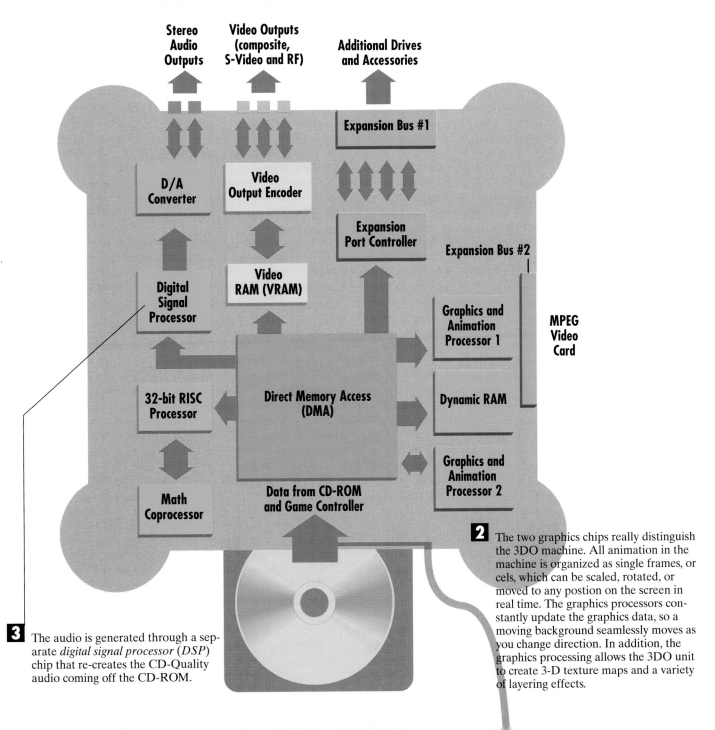

3 The audio is generated through a separate *digital signal processor* (*DSP*) chip that re-creates the CD-Quality audio coming off the CD-ROM.

2 The two graphics chips really distinguish the 3DO machine. All animation in the machine is organized as single frames, or cels, which can be scaled, rotated, or moved to any postion on the screen in real time. The graphics processors constantly update the graphics data, so a moving background seamlessly moves as you change direction. In addition, the graphics processing allows the 3DO unit to create 3-D texture maps and a variety of layering effects.

authoring

The process of integrating various media elements such as sound, video, and so on, to create an interactive program. *See Chapter 3.*

authoring system

The computers, software, and external hardware that multimedia developers use to create multimedia titles. *See Chapter 6.*

AVI (Audio Video Interleave)

AVI was developed by Microsoft to play back digital video on Windows-based machines. *See Chapter 4.*

CAV (Constant Angular Velocity)

CAV is a laser disc format used in most multimedia projects. The CAV format can hold up to 30 minutes of motion video or 54,000 still frames per side. *See Chapter 25.*

CD-I (Compact Disc-Interactive)

A proprietary CD-ROM player developed by Philips for playing back Green Book CD-ROM discs. *See Chapter 27.*

CD-R (Compact Disc-Recordable)

A CD-ROM format that enables you to record data onto a disc several times. Each time you record data is called a "session." To play back a multisession CD-R disc, you need a CD-ROM that is multisession compatible. *See Chapter 23.*

CD-ROM (Compact Disc Read-Only Memory)

An optical storage technology for storing and playing back computer data. *See Chapter 23.*

cel

A single frame of animation. *See Chapter 9.*

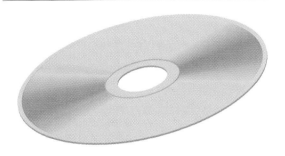

▶ **CD-ROM**

cel animation

The most common form of animation, where flat images are drawn one frame at a time. *See Chapter 9.*

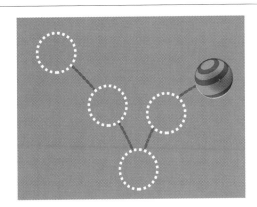

▶ **Cel animation**

CLV (Constant Linear Velocity)

CLV is a laser disc format that keeps the playback speed constant by changing the speed at which the disc revolves. CLV discs can hold 60 minutes of video per side, so you can store a two-hour program on a single disc. CLV lacks special features found with CAV discs, such as searching to a specific frame. *See Chapter 25.*

CODEC (Compressor/Decompressor algorithms)

A compression and decompression scheme that is used by system software (such as Apple's QuickTime extension) and external digitizing or playback hardware. *See Chapter 5.*

color depth

The actual number of colors used to display an image. Different monitor systems can display colors in 1 bit (black and white), 4 bits (16 colors), 8 bits (256 colors), 16 bits (32,768 colors), 24 bits (16.4 million colors), and 32 bits (16.4 million colors with 256 levels of transparency). *See Chapter 8.*

color palette

The number of colors available in an image. *See Chapter 8.*

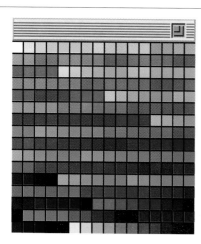

▸ **Color palette**

composite video

A standard video signal where the chrominance (color), luminance (brightness), and synchronization information are blended together in one signal. *See Chapter 15.*

CPU (Central Processing Unit)

The main brain of a computer system. *See Chapter 6.*

DAT (Digital Audio Tape)

A 4mm tape-based digital storage medium used in both audio and computer applications. *See Chapter 7.*

data throughput

The speed at which internal and external devices can transfer data to and from a computer. *See Chapter 7.*

▸ **Drive array**

drive array

A storage system that uses two or more hard disks in tandem, so that data throughput and access time are increased. *See Chapter 7.*

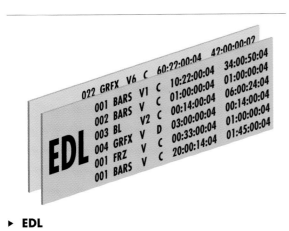

▶ **EDL**

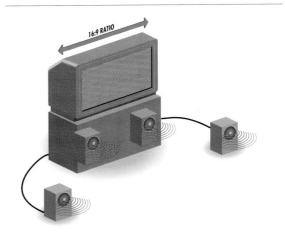

▶ **HDTV**

EDL (Edit Decision List)

An EDL is a record of every edit made in the off-line editing session. An EDL usually includes the start, stop, duration, and type of each edit. *See Chapter 15.*

field

Half of the lines in a video frame. The first field of the frame contains all of the odd-numbered lines in the frame, while the second field contains all the even lines. *See Part 4.*

frame

A single still image in both film and television. *See Part 4.*

generations

When applied to videotape technology, "generations" means the number of times that original videotape footage has been copied. *See Part 4.*

Green Book

A CD-ROM format developed by Philips for their CD-I system. Green Book discs can only be played back on CD-I players. *See Chapter 23.*

HDTV (High Definition Television)

The latest evolution of video, HDTV is a digital video signal that uses a wide-screen 16:9 image ratio, four channels of CD-quality audio, and double the resolution of regular video. *See Chapter 16.*

High Sierra

A subset of the Yellow Book standard, the High Sierra format was an attempt to create a worldwide standard for CD-ROM discs. It was later refined into the ISO 9660 format for Windows and DOS CD-ROM systems. *See Chapter 23.*

Indeo

Originally called DVI (Digital Video Interactive), this is a video compression format developed by Intel that is primarily designed to be a video distribution format. *See Chapter 14.*

interframe

A type of image compression found in MPEG video digitizing systems that removes redundant information in between frames to improve compression. *See Chapter 14.*

interlaced video

A video signal that uses two alternating fields per frame to create a video image. This is the standard format for television sets. *See Part 4.*

intraframe

A type of image compression found in JPEG and MPEG video digitizing systems that removes redundant information within each video frame to improve compression. *See Chapter 14.*

ISO (International Standards Organization) 9660

A subset of the Yellow Book standard, the ISO 9660 format is a worldwide standard for computer CD-ROM discs and is the most popular format for Windows and DOS CD-ROM systems. *See Chapter 23.*

JPEG (Joint Photographic Experts Group)

A still image compression system that reduces the size of a digital image file by using an intraframe compression scheme, where redundant information is thrown away. When used in conjunction with custom hardware, JPEG can compress and decompress images fast enough to display video at 30 frames per second. *See Chapter 13.*

key frame

A frame in both 2-D and 3-D animation that marks the position and movement of objects in a frame. A key frame in 3-D animation also contains the tilts and scale of each model in the key frame. *See Chapter 10.*

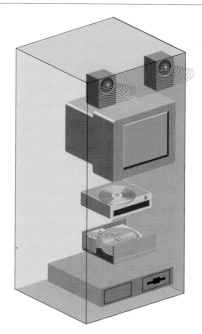

▶ **Kiosk**

kiosk

A stand-alone multimedia playback system used as a public information center. Kiosks often use touch screens instead of using keyboards or mice as input devices. *See Chapter 20.*

lossless compression

A compression scheme that never loses information when a file is compressed. This is the least effective form of compression for images. See *Chapter 13.*

lossy compression

A compression scheme in which some image information is lost each time the file is compressed. Most JPEG algorithms are lossy compression algorithms. See *Chapter 13.*

magneto-optical (MO) technology

A type of optical storage technology that uses lasers to write data onto a recordable optical surface. You can record data as many times as you like onto an MO disc, unlike CD-ROMs. *See Chapter 7.*

MCI (Media Control Interface)

Windows software that allows Windows-based computers to control external devices, such as CD-ROMs, VCRs, and laser disc players. *See Chapter 4.*

MIDI (Musical Instrument Digital Interface)

A communications standard created by electronic musical equipment vendors that defines a way for computer music programs, synthesizers, and other electronic equipment to exchange information and control signals. *See Chapter 19.*

MIDI interface

The link between personal computers and MIDI-compatible instruments. *See Chapter 19.*

modeling

The first step in three-dimensional animation, where the three-dimensional object is created. *See Chapter 10.*

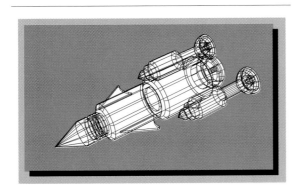

▶ **Modeling**

morphing

A special effect that takes two images and seamlessly changes one image into another. *See Chapter 11.*

▶ **Morphing**

MPC (Multimedia Personal Computer)

A hardware standard for IBM PCs and compatibles developed by Microsoft and other manufacturers. The MPC sets a standard hardware platform for playing back multimedia titles. *See Chapter 6.*

MPEG (Motion Picture Experts Group)

A moving-image compression standard that can compress video more than JPEG and still maintain a high image quality. MPEG uses an interframe compression scheme: Only one frame every half second is fully recorded, and only the changes between frames are then noted. *See Chapter 14.*

noninterlaced

A video signal that displays the image in just one scan without splitting up the frames. This is the standard system used in computer monitor displays. *See Chapter 14.*

NTSC (National Television Standards Committee)

This was the organization that set the standards for both the initial black-and-white video signal and later the color video standard. This is also used as a synonym for composite video. *See Chapter 15.*

off-line edit

The editing stage where copies of the original footage are used to try out ideas before completing the final project. It is during the off-line edit that an EDL is created. *See Chapter 15.*

on-line edit

The final stage of video editing, where the final production is edited together using the original raw footage in a high-end post-production facility called an on-line suite. *See Chapter 15.*

OOP (Object-Oriented Programming)

A modular programming language such as Kaleida's ScriptX that uses a building block approach to programming. *See Chapter 3.*

Orange Book

A CD format developed to define media for recordable CD drives. *See Chapter 23.*

PhotoCD

A proprietary image storage system developed by Kodak for recording photographs and slides onto an Orange Book CD. *See Chapter 23.*

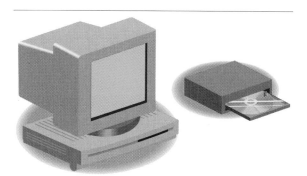

▸ **Playback system**

playback system

A personal computer system that contains the minimum level of hardware and software to play back multimedia titles. *See Chapter 6.*

QuickTime

The system software developed by Apple that can serve as a container for many types of media, such as video, audio, and animation. QuickTime contains compression, decompression, and synchronization systems for various types of media. *See Chapter 5.*

RAM (Random-Access Memory)
Where a computer's CPU keeps data for fast access. Unlike all other types of storage, data contained in RAM exists only as long as the computer is turned on. When the power is shut off, all data in RAM is lost. *See Chapter 6.*

Red Book
Also called CD-DA, the Red Book standard was the first compact disc format created by Sony and Philips for storing digital audio data. All audio compact discs use the Red Book CD format. *See Chapter 23.*

rendering
The final stage in the 3-D animation process, where the 3-D animation software blends together all the light sources, background images, texture maps, and surface attributes in the 3-D model. *See Chapter 10.*

RIFF (Resource Interchange File Format)
A standard file format for multimedia data on IBM PCs and compatibles; it can include bitmapped graphics, animation, digital audio, and MIDI files. *See Chapter 4.*

RISC (Reduced Instruction Set Computing)
A new type of high-powered processing chip found in Apple's PowerPC Mac computers and in 3DO machines. *See Chapter 6.*

sampling
The process that changes regular analog video or audio into a binary data structure of 1's and 0's that exists in all computer media. *See Chapter 12.*

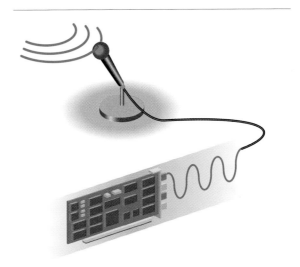

▶ Sampling

ScriptX
An object-oriented authoring language from Kaleida Labs that also acts as a multiplatform standard for multimedia software development. *See Chapter 3.*

SMPTE (Society of Motion Picture and Television Engineers)
A committee that sets standards for a wide variety of video and film production issues. They are most famous for SMPTE time code, a standard for defining the location of individual frames on a videotape. *See Chapter 15.*

source deck
In an edit system, the videotape deck that plays back your raw footage. *See Chapter 15.*

spline-based modeling
A type of 3-D modeling that uses bezier curves to bend lines into more realistic, curved shapes. *See Chapter 10.*

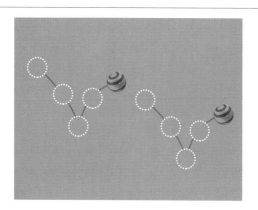

▶ **Sprites**

sprite

A mini-animation within an animation sequence. A good example of sprites are characters in video games that move across the screen. *See Chapter 9.*

S-Video or Y/C

A video format used in S-VHS and Hi-8mm video systems that separates the luminance (Y) and the chrominance (C) of the signal to improve image quality. Unlike component video, S-Video does not keep each of the three primary color signals separate. *See Part 4.*

▶ **Texture map**

texture map

A graphic image that is wrapped over the surface of a 3-D model to give the illusion that the texture is the outside skin of the object. Texture maps can add a wood, steel, or other surface look to 3-D models. *See Chapter 10.*

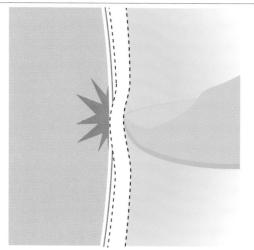

▶ **Touch screen**

touch screen

A device that enables you to control on-screen buttons by just pressing on a section of the screen. *See Chapter 20.*

VDIG (Video Digitizer)

A software driver created by third-party vendors for Apple's QuickTime software. A VDIG allows QuickTime to control any third-party hardware from within QuickTime. *See Chapter 5.*

vectors

A series of coordinate points that plots a three-dimensional model's location in three-dimensional animation. *See Chapter 10.*

Video CD-ROM

A new CD-ROM standard (also known as White Book) by Sony, Philips, and other manufacturers that uses MPEG compression to store up to 74 minutes of digital video on one CD-ROM. *See Chapter 23.*

Video For Windows

A digital video compression and decompression system developed by Microsoft for Windows-based personal computers. *See Chapter 12.*

video-on-demand

A future type of pay-per-view video service where you get to select both the show you want to watch and when you want to watch it. *See Part 4.*

VRAM (Video RAM)

RAM memory used specifically for graphic display functions such as increasing color depth. *See Chapter 15.*

warping

A variation on morphing special effects, where only one image changes over time. *See Chapter 11.*

Xcommands or Xobjects

Small custom pieces of code that are used to speed up commands or add special functions to an authoring program. *See Chapter 3.*

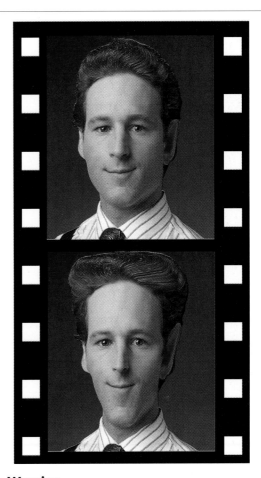

▶ **Warping**

Yellow Book

A CD-ROM format that is a variation on the Red Book audio CD format brought out by Sony and Philips. The Yellow Book format can hold computer data and contains much more complex data error correction programs. *See Chapter 23.*

ATTENTION TEACHERS AND TRAINERS
Now You Can Teach From These Books!

ZD Press now offers instructors and trainers
the materials they need to use these books in their classes.

- An Instructor's Manual features flexible lessons designed for use in a 10- or 15-week course (30-45 course hours).

- Student exercises and tests on floppy disk provide you with an easy way to tailor and/or duplicate tests as you need them.

- A Transparency Package contains all the graphics from the book, each on a single, full-color transparency.

- Spanish edition of *PC/Computing How Computers Work* will be available.

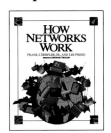

Imagination.
Innovation. Insight.

The How It Works Series from Ziff-Davis Press

"... a magnificently seamless integration of text and graphics ..."

Larry Blasko, The Associated Press, reviewing *PC/Computing How Computers Work*

No other books bring computer technology to life like the *How It Works* series from Ziff-Davis Press. Lavish, full-color illustrations and lucid text from some of the world's top computer commentators make *How It Works* books an exciting way to explore the inner workings of PC technology.

ISBN: 094-7 Price: $22.95

PC/Computing How Computers Work

A worldwide blockbuster that hit the general trade bestseller lists! *PC/Computing* magazine executive editor Ron White dismantles the PC and reveals what really makes it tick.

How Networks Work

Two of the most respected names in connectivity showcase the PC network, illustrating and explaining how each component does its magic and how they all fit together.

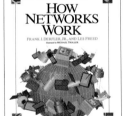

ISBN: 129-3 Price: $24.95

How Macs Work

A fun and fascinating voyage to the heart of the Macintosh! Two noted *MacUser* contributors cover the spectrum of Macintosh operations from startup to shutdown.

How Software Works

This dazzlingly illustrated volume from Ron White peeks inside the PC to show in full-color how software breathes life into the PC. Covers Windows™ and all major software categories.

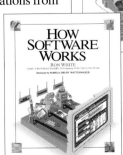

ISBN: 133-1 Price: $24.95

How to Use Your Computer

Conquer computerphobia and see how this intricate machine truly makes life easier. Dozens of full-color graphics showcase the components of the PC and explain how to interact with them.

All About Computers

This one-of-a-kind visual guide for kids features numerous full-color illustrations and photos on every page, combined with dozens of interactive projects that reinforce computer basics, making this an exciting way to learn all about the world of computers.

How To Use Word

Make Word 6.0 for Windows Work for You!

A uniquely visual approach puts the basics of Microsoft's latest Windows-based word processor right before the reader's eyes. Colorful examples invite them to begin producing a variety of documents, quickly and easily. Truly innovative!

ISBN: 184-6 Price: $17.95

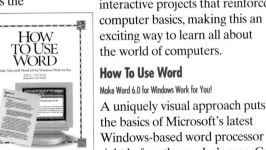

ISBN: 146-3 Price: $24.95

How To Use Excel

Make Excel 5.0 for Windows Work for You!

Covering the latest version of Excel, this visually impressive resource guides beginners to spreadsheet fluency through a full-color graphical approach that makes powerful techniques seem plain as day. Hands-on "Try It" sections give new users a chance to sharpen newfound skills.

ISBN: 155-2 Price: $22.95

ISBN: 166-8 Price: $15.95

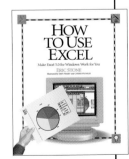

ISBN: 185-4 Price: $17.95

Available at all fine bookstores or by calling 1-800-688-0448, ext. 100. Call for more information on the Instructor's Supplement, including transparencies for each book in the *How It Works* Series.

The Quick and Easy Way to Learn.

Teaches DOS 6
The Quick and Easy Way to Learn

ISBN: 1-56276-100-5
Price: $22.95

Teaches WordPerfect 6.0
The Quick and Easy Way to Learn

ISBN: 1-56276-105-6
Price: $22.95

Teaches Word 6.0 for Windows
The Quick and Easy Way to Learn

ISBN: 1-56276-139-0
Price: $22.95

We know that PC Learning Labs books are the fastest and easiest way to learn because years have been spent perfecting them. Beginners will find practice sessions that are easy to follow and reference information that is easy to find. Even the most computer-shy readers can gain confidence faster than they ever thought possible.

The time we spent designing this series translates into time saved for you. You can feel confident that the information is accurate and presented in a way that allows you to learn quickly and effectively.

Teaches Microsoft Access
The Quick and Easy Way to Learn

ISBN: 1-56276-122-6
Price: $22.95

Teaches FoxPro 2.5 for Windows
The Quick and Easy Way to Learn

ISBN: 1-56276-176-5
Price: $22.95

Teaches OS/2 2.1
The Quick and Easy Way to Learn

ISBN: 1-56276-148-X
Price: $22.95

Teaches cc:Mail
The Quick and Easy Way to Learn

ISBN: 1-56276-135-8
Price: $22.95

Teaches WordPerfect 6.0 for Windows
The Quick and Easy Way to Learn

ISBN: 1-56276-020-3
Price: $22.95

Teaches Ami Pro 3.0
The Quick and Easy Way to Learn

ISBN: 1-56276-134-X
Price: $22.95

Teaches Microsoft Project 3.0 for Windows
The Quick and Easy Way to Learn

ISBN: 1-56276-124-2
Price: $22.95

Teaches Excel 4.0 for Windows
The Quick and Easy Way to Learn

ISBN: 1-56276-074-2
Price: $22.95

Teaches 1-2-3 Release 2.3

ISBN: 1-56276-033-5
Price: $22.95

Teaches Windows 3.1
The Quick and Easy Way to Learn

ISBN: 1-56276-051-3
Price: $22.95

Teaches PowerPoint for Windows
The Quick and Easy Way to Learn

ISBN: 1-56276-154-4
Price: $22.95

Teaches Lotus Notes 3.0
The Quick and Easy Way to Learn

ISBN: 1-56276-138-2
Price: $22.95

ZIFF DAVIS ZD PRESS

Also available: Titles featuring new versions of Excel, 1-2-3, Access, Microsoft Project, Ami Pro, and new applications, pending software release. Call 1-800-688-0448 for title update information.

Available at all fine bookstores, or by calling 1-800-688-0448, ext. 103.

Cut Here

Cut Here

Ziff-Davis Press Survey of Readers

Please help us in our effort to produce the best books on personal computing.
For your assistance, we would be pleased to send you a FREE catalog
featuring the complete line of Ziff-Davis Press books.

1. How did you first learn about this book?

Recommended by a friend . . . . ☐ -1 (5)

Recommended by store personnel . . . .☐ -2

Saw in Ziff-Davis Press catalog . . . .☐ -3

Received advertisement in the mail . . . .☐ -4

Saw the book on bookshelf at store . . . .☐ -5

Read book review in: _____ ☐ -6

Saw an advertisement in: _____ ☐ -7

Other (Please specify): _____ ☐ -8

2. Which THREE of the following factors most influenced your decision to purchase this book? (Please check up to THREE.)

Front or back cover information on book . . .☐ -1 (6)

Logo of magazine affiliated with book . . . . . .☐ -2

Special approach to the content . . . .☐ -3

Completeness of content . . . .☐ -4

Author's reputation. . . . .☐ -5

Publisher's reputation . . . .☐ -6

Book cover design or layout . . . .☐ -7

Index or table of contents of book . . . .☐ -8

Price of book . . . .☐ -9

Special effects, graphics, illustrations . . . . . .☐ -0

Other (Please specify): _____ ☐ -x

3. How many computer books have you purchased in the last six months? _____ (7-10)

4. On a scale of 1 to 5, where 5 is excellent, 4 is above average, 3 is average, 2 is below average, and 1 is poor, please rate each of the following aspects of this book below. (Please circle your answer.)

Depth/completeness of coverage	5	4	3	2	1	(11)
Organization of material	5	4	3	2	1	(12)
Ease of finding topic	5	4	3	2	1	(13)
Special features/time saving tips	5	4	3	2	1	(14)
Appropriate level of writing	5	4	3	2	1	(15)
Usefulness of table of contents	5	4	3	2	1	(16)
Usefulness of index	5	4	3	2	1	(17)
Usefulness of accompanying disk	5	4	3	2	1	(18)
Usefulness of illustrations/graphics	5	4	3	2	1	(19)
Cover design and attractiveness	5	4	3	2	1	(20)
Overall design and layout of book	5	4	3	2	1	(21)
Overall satisfaction with book	5	4	3	2	1	(22)

5. Which of the following computer publications do you read regularly; that is, 3 out of 4 issues?

Byte . . . .☐ -1 (23)

Computer Shopper . . . .☐ -2

Corporate Computing . . . .☐ -3

Dr. Dobb's Journal . . . .☐ -4

LAN Magazine . . . .☐ -5

MacWEEK . . . .☐ -6

MacUser . . . .☐ -7

PC Computing . . . .☐ -8

PC Magazine . . . .☐ -9

PC WEEK . . . .☐ -0

Windows Sources . . . .☐ -x

Other (Please specify): _____ ☐ -y

Please turn page.

Cut Here

6. What is your level of experience with personal computers? With the subject of this book?

	With PCs	With subject of book
Beginner	☐ -1 (24)	☐ -1 (25)
Intermediate	☐ -2	☐ -2
Advanced	☐ -3	☐ -3

7. Which of the following best describes your job title?

Officer (CEO/President/VP/owner) ☐ -1 (26)

Director/head ☐ -2

Manager/supervisor ☐ -3

Administration/staff ☐ -4

Teacher/educator/trainer ☐ -5

Lawyer/doctor/medical professional ☐ -6

Engineer/technician ☐ -7

Consultant ☐ -8

Not employed/student/retired ☐ -9

Other (Please specify): _____ ☐ -0

8. What is your age?

Under 20 ☐ -1 (27)

21-29 ☐ -2

30-39 ☐ -3

40-49 ☐ -4

50-59 ☐ -5

60 or over ☐ -6

9. Are you:

Male ☐ -1 (28)

Female ☐ -2

Thank you for your assistance with this important information! Please write your address below to receive our free catalog.

Name: _____

Address: _____

City/State/Zip: _____

Fold here to mail.

2087-03-08

_____

_____

_____

NO POSTAGE
NECESSARY
IF MAILED IN
THE UNITED
STATES

BUSINESS REPLY MAIL

FIRST CLASS MAIL   PERMIT NO. 1612   OAKLAND, CA

POSTAGE WILL BE PAID BY ADDRESSEE

Ziff-Davis Press
5903 Christie Avenue
Emeryville, CA 94608-1925
Attn: Marketing